A CourseGuide for

Historical Theology

Gregg R. Allison

ZONDERVAN ACADEMIC

A CourseGuide for Historical Theology

Copyright © 2019 by Zondervan

Requests for information should be addressed to:
Zondervan, *3900 Sparks Dr. SE, Grand Rapids, Michigan 49546*

ISBN 978-0-310-11116-0 (softcover)

All Scripture quotations, unless otherwise indicated, are taken from The Holy Bible, New International Version®, NIV®. Copyright © 1973, 1978, 1984, 2011 by Biblica, Inc.® Used by permission of Zondervan. All rights reserved worldwide. www.Zondervan.com. The "NIV" and "New International Version" are trademarks registered in the United States Patent and Trademark Office by Biblica, Inc.®

Any internet addresses (websites, blogs, etc.) and telephone numbers in this book are offered as a resource. They are not intended in any way to be or imply an endorsement by Zondervan, nor does Zondervan vouch for the content of these sites and numbers for the life of this book.

No part of this publication may be reproduced, stored in a retrieval system, or transmitted in any form or by any means — electronic, mechanical, photocopy, recording, or any other — except for brief quotations in printed reviews, without the prior permission of the publisher.

Printed in the United States of America

CONTENTS

Introduction 5

1. Introduction to Historical Theology 7
2. The Canon of Scripture 10
3. The Inspiration of Scripture 14
4. The Authority of Scripture 18
5. The Inerrancy of Scripture 22
6. The Clarity of Scripture 26
7. The Sufficiency and Necessity of Scripture 30
8. The Interpretation of Scripture 34
9. The Existence and Knowledge of God 38
10. The Character of God 42
11. God in Three Persons: The Trinity 46
12. Creation 50
13. Providence 54
14. Angels, Satan, and Demons 58
15. The Creation and Nature of Humanity 62
16. Sin 66
17. The Person of Jesus Christ 70

18. The Atonement... 74

19. Resurrection and Ascension 78

20. The Holy Spirit 82

21. Election and Reprobation 86

22. Regeneration, Conversion, and Effective Calling.......... 90

23. Justification (Right Legal Standing before God)........... 94

24. Sanctification (Growth in Likeness to Christ) 98

25. The Perseverance of the Saints
    (Remaining a Christian)................................ 102

26. The Church: Its Nature, Its Marks, and Its Purposes 106

27. Church Government 110

28. Baptism 114

29. The Lord's Supper 118

30. Worship 122

31. Christ's Return and the Millennium..................... 126

32. The Final Judgment and Eternal Punishment 130

33. The New Heavens and New Earth 134

Introduction

Welcome to *A CourseGuide for Historical Theology*. These guides were created for formal and informal students alike who want to engage deeper in biblical, theological, or ministry studies. We hope this guide will provide an opportunity for you to grow not only in your understanding, but also in your faith.

How to Use This Guide

This guide is meant to be used in conjunction with the book *Historical Theology* and its corresponding videos, *Historical Theology Video Lectures*. After you have read each chapter in the book and watched the accompanying video lesson, the materials in this guide will help you review and assess what you have learned. Application-oriented questions are included as well.

Each CourseGuide has been individually designed to best equip you in your studies, but in general, you can expect the following components. Most CourseGuides begin every chapter with a "You Should Know" section, which highlights key terminology, people, and facts to remember. This section serves as a helpful summary for directing your studies. Reflection questions, typically two to three per chapter, prompt you to summarize key points you've learned. Discussion questions invite you to an even deeper level of engagement. Finally, most chapters will end with a short quiz to test your retention. You can find the answer key to each quiz at the bottom of the page following it.

For Further Study

CourseGuides accompany books and videos from some of the world's top biblical and theological scholars. They may be used independently, or in small groups or classrooms, offering quality instruction to equip students for academic and ministry pursuits. If you would like to engage in further study with Zondervan's CourseGuides, the full lineup may be viewed online. After completing your studies with *A CourseGuide for Historical Theology*, we recommend moving on to *A CourseGuide for Systematic Theology*, *A CourseGuide for Church History, Volume One*, and *A CourseGuide for Church History, Volume Two*.

CHAPTER 1

Introduction to Historical Theology

You Should Know

- Historical theology provides numerous benefits for Christians and today's church.

- While it is not infallible, historical theology plays a ministerial and helping role as it aids the church in its interpretation of Scripture.

- An essential Christian theology really does exist, and churches, through the aid of historical theology, can move closer to recognizing and affirming this sound doctrine.

- Along with historical theology, the theological task must include exegetical theology, biblical theology, systematic theology, and practical theology. Each of these other disciplines are informed and aided by historical theology.

- Historical theology: the study of the interpretation of Scripture and the formulation of doctrine by the church of the past

- Orthodoxy: that which the New Testament calls "sound doctrine"; that which rightly reflects in summary form all the teaching of Scripture and which the church is bound to believe and obey

- Heresy: anything that contradicts sound doctrine; it is false belief that misinterprets Scripture or ignores some of the teaching of Scripture, or that incorrectly puts together all the teaching of Scripture

- Essentialist approach: In truth, only one "correct" Christianity has been handed down, and all others are erroneous and deviant.

- Moderate essentialist approach: A center, a core, of Christian doctrine, does exist, but it does not manifest itself in any one particular church or theological movement.

- Relativist approach: The development of doctrine over the course of the centuries exhibits such an immense diversity that it is not possible to identify a core, or essential center, of the Christian faith.

Essay Questions

Short

1. What is the proper relationship between Scripture and tradition?

2. How does the divine promise that Christ will be with his church affect the human work of building a theology?

3. What is the moderate essentialist perspective, and how does it contrast with the relativist and the extreme essentialist perspectives?

Long

1. Are there specific, modern-day heresies that historical theology can help the church to avoid? Name three, and then explain how historical theology might address them.

Quiz

1. (T/F) In determining doctrine and practice, the magisterial, or authoritative, role belongs to historical theology, while the ministerial and helping role belongs to Scripture alone.

2. (T/F) One benefit of historical theology is that it encourages the church to focus on those areas that have *not* been emphasized regularly throughout the history of the church.

3. (T/F) The relativist notion that there is no core or essential character to the Christian faith is to be rejected.

4. (T/F) Historical theology is considered infallible.

5. (T/F) The study of historical theology is said to promote personal autonomy and individualism in the theological enterprise.

6. (T/F) Orthodoxy is defined as anything that contradicts sound doctrine. It is false belief that misinterprets Scripture, or that ignores some of the teaching of Scripture, or that incorrectly puts together all the teaching of Scripture.

7. (T/F) Historical theology is the study of the interpretation of Scripture and the formulation of doctrine by the church of the past.

8. In its approach to historical theology, this book takes a(n) _____ approach.
   a) Subchronic
   b) Diachronic
   c) Anachronic
   d) Synchronic

9. Which three disciplines deal *directly* with Scripture and thus constitute the important interpretive and organizational process in constructing theology?
   a) Historical theology, exegetical theology, and biblical theology
   b) Exegetical theology, biblical theology, and systematic theology
   c) Biblical theology, systematic theology, and practical theology
   d) Systematic theology, practical theology, and historical theology

10. Which of the following is *not* listed as one of the benefits of historical theology?
    a) It encourages the church to focus on the essentials of the faith.
    b) It gives the church hope by providing assurance that Jesus is fulfilling his promise to his people.
    c) It privileges the church to enjoy a sense of belonging to the church of the past.
    d) It stands as the fundamental basis for authority which the church can look to for truth.

ANSWER KEY

1. F, 2. F, 3. T, 4. F, 5. F, 6. F, 7. T, 8. B, 9. B, 10. D

CHAPTER 2

The Canon of Scripture

You Should Know

- Josephus considered the Hebrew canon to be closed after the writings of Ezra, Nehemiah, and Esther (435 BC), since there was no longer any prophetic witness.

- All of the Old Testament books that are considered canonical today were present and together composed the Word of God for the Jewish people — and the early church.

- Two criteria for the acceptance of books into the New Testament canon were antiquity and apostolicity.

- The Apocrypha has historically been accepted by the Roman Catholic Church and rejected by Protestants as authoritative Scripture.

- The humanist motto "*ad fontes*" and the Reformation principle "*sola Scriptura*" were instrumental in recovering the authority of the original Hebrew Old Testament and Greek New Testament Scriptures.

- Some modern scholars have questioned the traditional formulations of the canon through the employment of the historical-critical method.

- Montanism, a heresy of the early church, was a movement that encouraged an eager anticipation of the Lord's quick return by appealing to new revelations given by the Holy Spirit. The church responded to this emphasis on revelation outside of the Bible by underscoring the closed canon of Scripture.

- Erasmus, a leading humanist scholar, insisted that the Latin Vulgate translation of Matthew 4:17 was incorrectly translated.

Instead of the Vulgate version, which read "do penance," he suggested that the Greek should be translated "repent."

- Athanasius's New Testament canon was officially endorsed by the Council of Hippo in AD 393.

- Beginning in the third century before Christ, a Greek translation of the Hebrew Bible called the Septuagint was undertaken.

Essay Questions

Short

1. What are some of the early witnesses to the authority of the New Testament writings?

2. What principle did the Reformers assert against the supremacy of the Roman Catholic Church, and what effect did it have?

3. What was the effect of historical criticism on the canon? What influence did Brevard Childs have on evangelical understandings of the canon?

Long

1. What criteria enabled the early church to define Scripture, and how did those criteria function (i.e., to determine vs. to recognize inspired Scripture)? Briefly summarize and explain that criteria.

Quiz

1. (T/F) In a series of letters between them, Augustine urged Jerome to translate the Old Testament into Latin from the Hebrew rather than from the Septuagint.

2. (T/F) At the Council of Hippo the Roman Catholic Church sought to correct the Protestant "errors" by reaffirming the Catholic canon of Scripture, which included the apocryphal writings.

3. (T/F) In AD 382 Jerome set out to produce a Latin translation of the Bible, called the *Latin Vulgate*, which would stand as the church's Bible for over a millennium.

4. (T/F) Books of the Bible including James, 2 Peter, 2 and 3 John, Jude, and Hebrews were unanimously accepted as canonical without exception.

5. (T/F) The formal principle of the Reformers and Protestantism was *sola Scriptura*, which meant that biblical Scripture, because it is the Word of God, has the authority and credibility to stand on its own without the need of the church to confer authority on it.

6. What developed in the medieval period that set the stage for an unraveling of the nearly one-thousand-year consensus with regard to Scripture's canon?
    a) The rise of the movement called humanism
    b) The Historical Critical Method
    c) The discovery of the Muratorian Fragment
    d) The French Confession of Faith

7. _____ was a leader of a heretical movement that promoted a "canon" of Scripture that consisted of "the Gospel and the Apostle" (a mutilated version of the gospel of Luke and ten letters of Paul). He rejected the entire Old Testament and all parts of the growing New Testament that reflected favorably upon the Old.
    a) Friedrich Schleiermacher
    b) Montanus
    c) Marcion
    d) Herman Ridderbos

8. The first appearance of a list of New Testament writings that corresponds exactly with the canon as is known today was _____.
    a) Irenaeus's *Against Heresies*
    b) L. A. Muratori's *Antiquitates Italicae Medii Aevi*
    c) Eusebius's *Ecclesiastical History*
    d) Athanasius's *Thirty-Ninth Easter Letter*

9. The Latin expression "*ad fontes*" was humanism's motto that meant _____.

   a) "Back to the sources"
   b) "Adding to authority"
   c) "Scripture alone"
   d) "Fount of knowledge"

10. In the early church, which two key criteria emerged to determine the writings that would be included in the New Testament canon?

   a) Orthodoxy and notoriety
   b) Notoriety and antiquity
   c) Apostolicity and antiquity
   d) Apostolicity and orthodoxy

ANSWER KEY

1. F, 2. F, 3. T, 4. F, 5. T, 6. A, 7. C, 8. D, 9. A, 10. C

CHAPTER 3

The Inspiration of Scripture

You Should Know

- The church has historically believed that all the words of Scripture are "God-breathed" such that the Bible is the actual Word of God.

- Only in the modern period has this doctrine come under attack, though most evangelicals still cling to and defend it.

- Friedrich Schleiermacher was a pivotal figure in the modern era of Protestant thought. Seeking to completely reformulate the doctrine of inspiration, he rooted personal faith in a personal experience of Jesus Christ that was not dependent on an inspired Bible.

- Karl Barth made a distinction between the Bible and the Word of God, maintaining that the Bible is simply a witness to revelation and that it becomes the Word of God.

- In response to a wide array of attacks, evangelicals have sought to defend the historical doctrine of the inspiration of Scripture. The evangelical consensus was finally expressed in the Chicago Statement on Biblical Inerrancy, which upheld the verbal plenary inspiration of Scripture, rejected the mechanical dictation theory, and affirmed Scripture's inerrancy.

- Jack Rogers and Donald McKim made a distinction between the infallibility of Scripture and the inerrancy of Scripture; they embraced the former as being a property of Scripture and rejected the latter because of its novelty.

- John Quenstedt and John Gerhard articulated a distinction between the divine and human authors of Scripture, calling God the *efficient cause* of Scripture and holy men of God the *instrumental causes* of Scripture.

- Friedrich Schleiermacher relegated the Old Testament to secondary status in the Bible and suggested that it did not share normative dignity or inspiration with the rest of Scripture.

- Verbal-plenary inspiration: the theory of inspiration that accurately represents the historical position of the church that Scripture is *fully* inspired, even to its very *words*

- Confluence: the term used by B. B. Warfield to speak of the divine-human cooperation that takes place when the Spirit of God works along with the providentially and graciously determined work of men to produce an inspired Scripture

Essay Questions

Short

1. What was the consensus view concerning inspiration in the early church?

2. Why is Calvin sometimes thought to promote a dictation theory of inspiration, and is this understanding of his teaching accurate? What role does the witness of the Spirit play in Calvin's understanding of inspiration?

3. Why does Barth want to separate the Bible as witness to revelation from revelation itself?

Long

1. Explain and summarize the doctrine expressed in the two main passages that provide the biblical account of inspiration, 2 Timothy 3:16 and 2 Peter 1:19–21.

Quiz

1. (T/F) The doctrine of the inspiration of Scripture has been a subject of much contention and disagreement throughout the history of the church, especially in the early church.

2. (T/F) John Calvin rejected the notion of a superintending work of the Holy Spirit in the production of the Word of God.

3. (T/F) Hippolytus rejected the idea that biblical writers were entirely passive instruments being played by a divine musician to pen the words of Scripture.

4. (T/F) John Calvin argued for a form of the mechanical dictation theory of inspiration.

5. (T/F) According to the *Westminster Confession of Faith*, the translations of Scripture are directly inspired by God.

6. _____ was a theory of inspiration which suggested that biblical writers were mere secretaries recording word for word what the Holy Spirit told them to write.
   a) Confluence
   b) Mechanical dictation
   c) Verbal-plenary inspiration
   d) *Theopneustos*

7. _____ was pivotal in bringing an altered concept of the inspiration of Scripture into Protestantism. He completely reformulated the doctrine of inspiration to bring it in line with his view that the Christian religion is a feeling of absolute dependence on God. He further presented a case that faith cannot be grounded on a foundation of Scripture proven to be inspired by God. According to him, faith must arise from an experience of Jesus Christ related only minimally to the Bible.
   a) Charles Hartshorne
   b) Immanuel Kant
   c) Horace Bushnell
   d) Friedrich Schleiermacher

8. _____ has become the standard and common expression of evangelicalism's doctrine of inspiration.

   a) B. B. Warfield's "The Church Doctrine of Inspiration"
   b) The *Westminster Confession of Faith*
   c) The *Chicago Statement on Biblical Inerrancy*
   d) Basil Manly Jr.'s *The Bible Doctrine of Inspiration*

9. According to the *Westminster Confession*, the divine inspiration of Scripture along with its providentially protected transmission should be accompanied by _____.

   a) Translation
   b) Biblical criticism
   c) Scholarship
   d) Evangelism

10. The pre-Reformer _____ identified God with his Word so closely that he said, "[God] and his Word are all one, and they may not be separated."

   a) John Gerhard
   b) John Wycliffe
   c) John Quenstedt
   d) John Calvin

ANSWER KEY

1. F, 2. F, 3. T, 4. F, 5. F, 6. B, 7. D, 8. C, 9. A, 10. B

CHAPTER 4

The Authority of Scripture

You Should Know

- The church has historically acknowledged that all the words in Scripture are God's words in such a way that to believe and obey the Bible is to believe and obey God himself.

- In the early church, appeal to tradition was never intended to deprive Scripture of its rightful place of authority, but rather it functioned as a support for the proper understanding of authoritative Scripture against heretical claims.

- For its first millennium and more, the church affirmed the supreme authority of Scripture, but during the latter part of the Middle Ages the Roman Catholic Church permitted other sources to lay claim to the title of authoritative truth. A multiple-source notion arose, including Scripture, church tradition, and the teaching office of the church.

- In response to Rome, Martin Luther championed the formal Protestant and Reformation principle *sola Scriptura*, which presented Scripture as the final judge of Christian doctrine and practice, standing above everything and everyone else.

- A growing tide of biblical criticism, rooted in a denial of the divine inspiration and truthfulness of Scripture, has slowly diminished people's traditional confidence in the authority of Scripture.

- Emil Brunner substituted the authority of the Bible with the authority of Jesus Christ. Convinced in his conscience that Jesus

Christ is the Truth, he taught that one is "not required to believe the Scriptures because they are the Scriptures" but because Jesus meets him in the Scriptures.

- Posing a rather speculative, obscure, and innocuous set of theoretical questions, Henry of Ghent is credited with driving a wedge between the church's previously close correlation between the authority of the church and the authority of Scripture.

- Thomas Netter Waldensis, in his discussion of "oral tradition," introduced a new and controversial concept of apostolic succession as a guarantee of sound doctrine.

- A standard and common expression of evangelicalism's doctrine of the authority of Scripture, the Chicago Statement on Biblical Inerrancy has stood in the classic Protestant legacy affirming authority as an intrinsic property of Scripture.

- In its fight against heresy the early church often appealed to its own authority and tradition, though these were never regarded as supplements to or opponents of Scripture.

Essay Questions

Short

1. What two principles of biblical authority did Luther deduce from the formal principal of *sola Scriptura*?

2. What major development in the Roman Catholic understanding of authority and inspiration occurred in the early modern period?

3. What were the effects of Schleiermacher's emphasis on faith rather than Scripture as the basis of authority?

Long

1. Why should Christians acknowledge the authority of Scripture? How does the Bible attest to its own authority, and what are the various passages which support this testimony?

Quiz

1. (T/F) For its first millennium and more, the church affirmed the supreme authority of Scripture, but during the latter part of the Middle Ages the Roman Catholic Church permitted other sources to lay claim to the title of authoritative truth. A multiple-source notion arose, including Scripture, church tradition, and the teaching office of the church.

2. (T/F) Anselm championed human reason and philosophy as the highest authority above Scripture.

3. (T/F) Martin Luther taught that the authority of Scripture means that the preached word is to be regarded as the Word of God.

4. (T/F) Arguing against the Roman Catholic Church's two-source notion of divine authority, Charles Hodge averred that such an understanding logically leads to the demotion of scriptural authority and the elevation of the church's interpretation of Scripture.

5. During the _____ many considered the Scripture to be authoritative because of the way it *functions*.
   a) Early church
   b) Middle Ages
   c) Reformation and Post-Reformation
   d) Modern period

6. Clement of Alexandria viewed Scripture as authoritative because _____.
   a) It derives its status of authority from the church
   b) Of the way it functions
   c) In it the voice of God is heard
   d) Of the practical and pragmatic benefits

7. _____ insisted on the supremacy of Scripture over all human authority, including the pope.
   a) Albert Pigge
   b) John Hus
   c) John Eck
   d) John Cochlaus

8. The dogma of the infallibility of the pope was pronounced at
_____.

   a) the Council of Chalcedon
   b) the Council of Trent
   c) Vatican Council I
   d) Vatican Council II

9. Rather than saying that the Bible *is* the Word of God, _____ suggested that one should rather say that it *becomes* the Word of God, when God condescends sovereignly and freely to reveal himself to people through the Bible.

   a) John Quenstedt
   b) Emil Brunner
   c) Karl Barth
   d) D. Martyn Lloyd-Jones

10. In the fourteenth century, _____ formulated five categories of truth that the church must believe. According to him, one of these categories of truth has "come down to us from the apostles by word of mouth." This orally transmitted tradition from the apostles to the postapostolic church was a novel idea during this time.

    a) John Wycliffe
    b) William of Ockham
    c) Guido Terreni
    d) Gerald of Bologna

ANSWER KEY

1. T, 2. F, 3. T, 4. T, 5. D, 6. C, 7. B, 8. C, 9. C, 10. B

CHAPTER 5

The Inerrancy of Scripture

You Should Know

- The church has historically acknowledged that Scripture in its original manuscripts and properly interpreted is completely true and without any error in everything that it affirms, whether that has to do with doctrine, moral conduct, or matters of history, cosmology, geography, and the like.

- Following in line with its Jewish predecessors, the early church recognized the complete truthfulness of Scripture.

- The vast majority of theologians during the Middle Ages understood the Scriptures to be totally truthful.

- This same conviction of the inerrancy of Scripture continued throughout the Reformation and post-Reformation period. Martin Luther taught that the truthful Scripture corresponds with reality and that it never contradicts itself.

- With the rise of the scientific revolution and biblical criticism, the consensus concerning the inerrancy of Scripture that had been held throughout the history of the church began to deteriorate during the seventeenth century.

- Paul Feinberg formulated the definition for inerrancy that has become the standard view of conservative evangelicals in the twenty-first century.

- Known for his famous phrase "*Cogito, ergo sum* (I think, therefore I am)," René Descartes understood man, as a thinking subject, to be the starting point of human knowledge.

- Standing as an exception to the medieval consensus concerning the inerrancy of Scripture, Peter Abelard taught that "the prophets themselves sometimes lacked God's gift of prophecy and, by dint of their sheer practice in their craft, produced false prophecies, emanating from their own spirit, while all the time believing that they possessed the gift of prophesy."

- Known as the documentary hypothesis, this series of theories proposed that the Pentateuch was composed over about five centuries as a collection of selections from several written documents, written by several different authors in several different locations.

- Charles Darwin's work *Origin of Species* served to undermine people's confidence in the truthfulness of the creation account in Genesis.

Essay Questions

Short

1. What two corollaries did early Christians draw from the Bible's complete truthfulness?

2. The belief in inerrancy among early Protestant theologians, in addition to restating the common theology of the church, had to deal with a particular heresy. What was it and what were its claims?

3. How did the scientific revolution prepare people to accept the methods and conclusions of historical criticism?

Long

1. Summarize the key denials and affirmations of the *Chicago Statement on Biblical Inerrancy*. What specific clarifications does Paul Feinberg bring to the doctrine of inerrancy given in the *Chicago Statement on Biblical Inerrancy*?

Quiz

1. (T/F) For Thomas Aquinas, the salvation of fallen human beings depended on divine revelation being truthful and without error.

2. (T/F) Augustine taught that the presence of just one error in Scripture would not mean that all of Scripture is in error; instead, it would lead to the suspicion that any part could be in error. This would lead the church to the hopelessly subjective opinion to act as the judge of Scripture's truthfulness.

3. (T/F) Known for his work with Aristotle's philosophy, Thomas Aquinas affirmed theology to be more certain than any other disciple, except philosophy.

4. (T/F) Paul Feinberg argued against the common evangelical position that noted that statements of Scripture can be true even if they are grammatically incorrect.

5. (T/F) John Calvin taught that Moses avoided a technical, scientific account of the creation because his intent was to teach average people.

6. With his "pre-Adam" theory, _____ set off the conflict between theology and science.
   a) Isaac La Peyrère
   b) Richard Popkin
   c) Hugo Grotius
   d) Baruch Spinoza

7. Considered by many to be the "father of biblical criticism," _____ wrote against Baruch Spinoza's attack on Mosaic authorship of the Pentateuch.
   a) William Robertson Smith
   b) John Toland
   c) Richard Simon
   d) Jean Leclerc

8. The post-Reformation theologians' affirmation of truthfulness of Scripture was for the most part in reaction to a heretical movement

led by _____, which allowed for errors in portions of Scripture and suggested that because these were minor errors they had no effect on matters of salvation and doctrine.

   a) Hymenaeus
   b) Philetus
   c) Socinus
   d) Apollinaris

9. Known for his heliocentric theory, _____ showed that the sun rather than the earth was at the center of the solar system. His theory replaced Ptolemy's geocentric theory of the universe.

   a) Francis Bacon
   b) Nicolas Copernicus
   c) Galileo Galilei
   d) Johannes Kepler

10. A Jewish philosopher, _____ was greatly influenced by the philosophy of René Descartes. As a result, he insisted that human reason was the key criterion for true knowledge and that it stood above Scripture and even judges it. He, therefore, sought to apply this methodology to the study of Scripture.

    a) Matthew Poole
    b) Baruch Spinoza
    c) Hugo Grotius
    d) Solomon Steinheim

ANSWER KEY

1. T, 2. T, 3. F, 4. F, 5. T, 6. A, 7. C, 8. C, 9. B, 10. B

CHAPTER 6

The Clarity of Scripture

You Should Know

- The church has historically affirmed that the Bible is written in a way that its teachings are understandable by everyone who reads it, seeking God for his help and being willing to obey it.

- Apart from some who were influenced by Gnosticism, the majority of those in the early church affirmed the doctrine of the clarity of Scripture. Gnosticism was a heretical movement that promoted a mysterious or secret knowledge that was reserved for and was only accessible to elite members of the group.

- During the Middle Ages, the educated people of society tended to be priests. A natural separation began to form between the educated clergy and the uneducated laity. This distinction would develop into Roman Catholic dogma, as the church prohibited laity from being permitted to have the Scriptures.

- The clarity of Scripture became a major area of disagreement between the Roman Catholic Church and the Protestants. Defenses came from both sides of the argument.

- While this doctrine, in the modern age, has experienced opposition as a result of both the science of hermeneutics and higher biblical criticism, it has served as the foundation and motivation for the translation of the Scriptures into numerous languages as a part of the Protestant missionary endeavor. As a whole, the doctrine has been sorely neglected.

- While Origen taught that the Bible was clear to all believers whenever it addressed crucial truths, he also taught that the

Bible contained mystery such that even experts could not hope to understand fully the divine.

- In his *The Bondage of the Will*, written against the Christian humanist Erasmus, Martin Luther spelled out his view on the clarity of Scripture.

- The science of hermeneutics, the study of the rules of interpretation, stood as one of the trends in the modern period that served to undermine the doctrine of the clarity of Scripture.

- Although the medieval church decried the use of the Bible by laypeople, John Wycliffe, as a proponent of the clarity of Scripture, made it available in the language of the English people.

- The Roman Catholic Church emphasized the obscurity of Scripture for the laity and insisted that only its clergy could understand it rightly.

Essay Questions

Short

1. What principle of interpretation did Tertullian, and later Augustine, lay down for interpreting difficult passages? How did Augustine find positive value in those passages of Scripture that seem difficult and obscure?

2. What social and ecclesial factors of the medieval period contributed to the inability of people to understand the Scriptures on their own?

3. What does Allison mean by "the presumption of continued intelligibility" in his revision of the doctrine of Scripture's clarity?

Long

1. Summarize and explain Luther's twofold understanding of the clarity of Scripture. What were the consequences of the Reformers' insistence on the clarity of Scripture?

Quiz

1. (T/F) Augustine believed that the plainer passages of Scripture could be used to shed light upon the more obscure passages.

2. (T/F) Vying for a separation between clergy and laity, John Wycliffe was intent on ensuring that the laity should not be permitted to have the books of the Old and New Testaments in their common language.

3. (T/F) According to Martin Luther, if anyone had difficulty interpreting the text of the Bible, the error belonged to the human, not the Scripture.

4. (T/F) Huldrych Zwingli's ideas concerning the distinction between the *external Word* and the *internal Word* proved to be an important teaching throughout the Reformation and post-Reformation, since the other Reformers followed and continued to teach and follow Zwingli's ideas.

5. Being highly influenced by Gnosticism, _____ believed that any and all truth about God is inexpressible such that it is impossible to express God. His influence led to the formation of a two-tiered system of Christians, with spiritual believers being able to understand the mysteries of Scripture that simple believers could not appreciate.

   a) Gregory the Great
   b) Chrysostom
   c) Cyril of Alexandria
   d) Clement of Alexandria

6. Believing that all could benefit from teachings of the Bible _____ wrote, "In its obvious sense, it [Scripture] has food to nourish little ones. In its secret meaning, it can command the admiration of the most learned minds. It is almost like a river, both shallow and deep, in which a lamb may walk and an elephant swim."

   a) Cyril of Alexandria
   b) Origen
   c) Augustine
   d) Gregory the Great

7. At _____ it was decreed that the Latin Vulgate was the official version of Scripture.

   a) The Council of Toulouse
   b) The Council of Trent
   c) Vatican I
   d) Vatican II

8. In response to the Roman Catholic Church's claims to having the sole authority in interpreting the Bible the post-Reformers insisted on scriptural clarity concerning those things that are essential to the doctrine of _____.

   a) Church authority
   b) Salvation
   c) God
   d) Humanity

9. In the modern period, _____ served to take away the individual believer's ability to interpret the Bible for himself and forced many laypeople to doubt their own ability to understand anything.

   a) Higher biblical criticism
   b) Communal interpretive methods
   c) Church authority
   d) Gnosticism

10. According to _____, a distinction should be made between the *text* of Scripture and the *subject matter* of Scripture. The text may be obscure, but the subject matter is fully knowable.

    a) John Calvin
    b) John Gerhard
    c) Martin Luther
    d) Huldrych Zwingli

ANSWER KEY

1. T, 2. F, 3. T, 4. F, 5. D, 6. D, 7. B, 8. B, 9. A, 10. C

CHAPTER 7

The Sufficiency and Necessity of Scripture

You Should Know

- The church has historically affirmed both the doctrines of the sufficiency and the necessity of Scripture.

- The Bible, composed of both the Old and New Testaments, served as the sufficient source for authority, truth, doctrine, and practical instruction for life, faith, and obedience in the early church.

- What started with the early church fathers referring to other sources of Christian beliefs and practice—apostolic tradition, the canon of truth, and church authority—would prove to become the background for later controversies concerning the Bible.

- In the early part of the medieval period, the correlation between Scripture and the church's traditional biblical interpretation was not problematic, since it held to the sufficiency and necessity of Scripture. However, these doctrines came under attack and began to fade away completely in the latter part of the Middle Ages.

- The Roman Catholic Church came to affirm that Scripture is needed for the *bene esse* (well-being) but not the *esse* (existence) of the church.

- Martin Luther experienced resistance from two fronts: the Roman Catholic Church and the enthusiasts (or fanatics).

- The Methodist development known as the Wesleyan quadrilateral challenged the church's traditional understanding of the doctrines of the sufficiency and necessity of Scripture since it embraced four sources for theological understanding: Scripture, tradition, experience, and reason.

- The official Catholic objection to the Protestants' views concerning the sufficiency and necessity of Scripture was decreed at the Council of Trent.

- Charles Hodge attempted to develop a list of key doctrines categorized by the majority of Roman Catholic theologians as being incompletely revealed in Scripture. He concluded that the Catholic advocacy of tradition leads the Church "to depreciate the Scriptures, and to show how much the Church would lose if she had no other source of knowledge of divine truth but the written word."

- A general division among modern day evangelicals has grown and continues to grow between integrationists and strict Biblicists. The Biblicists insist that Scripture's sufficiency is undermined when biblical truth is combined with humanly derived knowledge.

Essay Questions

Short

1. Why was the sufficiency of Scripture an important element in the fight against heresy in the early church?

2. What arguments did Aquinas make to support the necessity of Scripture, even for doctrines that could be discovered through reason?

3. Explain how *sola Scriptura*, the formal principle of the Reformation, relates to the doctrine of Scripture's sufficiency.

Long

1. Grudem specifies several ways that the doctrine of the sufficiency and necessity of Scripture provide comfort to the believer today. Summarize and restate these in your own words.

Quiz

1. (T/F) The earliest church collectively affirmed the doctrine of the necessity of Scripture while rejecting the sufficiency of Scripture.

2. (T/F) The earliest Christians looked to the Jewish Bible as their sufficient source of doctrinal and practical instruction for a life of faith and obedience.

3. (T/F) Old and New Testament writers affirmed the sufficiency of Scripture.

4. (T/F) Clement of Alexandria understood the doctrine of the sufficiency of Scripture much like an axiom in math or a first principle in philosophy. That is, it has no need of proof.

5. (T/F) Referring to apostolic tradition, the canon of truth, and church authority as other sources for authority, the leaders in the early church began to diminish the doctrines of the sufficiency and necessity of Scripture as they had been received from their Jewish ancestors.

6. With the necessity of Scripture in mind, _____ rebuked Christians who thought they did not need the Bible because they were not monks: "This belief . . . has ruined you, because you need it much more than they do. For those who live in the world and each day are wounded are the ones who have the most need of medicine. . . . The things that are contained in Scripture — do you not think that they are highly necessary?"

   a) Gregory the Great
   b) Chrysostom
   c) Cyril of Alexandria
   d) Clement of Alexandria

7. _____ was a means of underscoring what true churches believed and a way of exposing groups that promoted heresy. It was a succinct expression of early church beliefs and was derived from Scripture itself.

   a) Apostolic tradition
   b) The canon of truth (or the rule of faith)

c) Church authority
d) The Augsburg Confession

8. Responding to objections to the doctrine of the sufficiency of Scripture including arguments concerning the progressive nature of revelation, superfluous ceremonies, and historical accounts in Scripture, _____ affirmed Scripture's sufficiency, citing Augustine's belief that canonical Scripture is supremely authoritative in "all matters of which we ought not to be ignorant, and yet cannot know of ourselves."

   a) William Whitaker
   b) Abraham Calov
   c) John Duns Scotus
   d) John Owen

9. It was the _____ position that Scripture is needed for the *bene esse* (well-being) of the church but not the *esse* (existence) of the church.

   a) Protestant
   b) Early church
   c) Integrationist
   d) Roman Catholic

10. The "perfection of Scripture" was the term used by the _____, which was used to designate both the sufficiency and necessity of Scripture.

   a) Early church
   b) Medieval church
   c) Reformers
   d) Post-Reformers

ANSWER KEY
1. F, 2. T, 3. T, 4. T, 5. F, 6. B, 7. B, 8. C, 9. D, 10. D

CHAPTER 8

The Interpretation of Scripture

You Should Know

- From the inception of the church, Christians have usually approached the interpretation of the Bible using either a literal or an allegorical method.

- During the early church, two major schools of thoughts developed. The school of Alexandria embraced a more allegorical approach to interpretation, and the school of Antioch embraced a more literal and typological approach.

- According to Origen, Scripture has three levels of meaning, which correspond to the three parts of human beings (who are composed of body, soul, and spirit).

- A distinction between an allegorical/multiple-senses approach and a more literal and typological approach continued during the Middle Ages. However, the Roman Catholic Church began to assert itself as the sole interpreter of Scripture.

- The Reformers insisted on a literal interpretive approach, emphasizing the important role of the Holy Spirit in illumining the reader in his hermeneutical work.

- The Roman Catholic Church responded to Protestants at the Council of Trent by making the Latin Vulgate the official version of Scripture that the church must use and also by declaring that the church possesses the sole right to interpret the Bible.

- Biblical criticism began to shake people's confidence in the truthfulness and authority of Scripture during the modern age, which led to great diversity and change in biblical interpretation.

- Evangelicals have continued to defend a more literal/typological approach while also seeking to present a more comprehensive approach to biblical interpretation.

- Typology: the method of interpretation that underscores the correspondence between what occurred in the Old Testament with something else that occurred in the New Testament

- Book of Rules: Tyconius' book that offers seven rules of biblical interpretation and stands as one of the earliest hermeneutical manuals in the church

Essay Questions

Short

1. What limits did Augustine attempt to place on the use of allegory? Do you think that these safeguards are sufficient?

2. What hermeneutical principles did Luther and Calvin share? Which ones were different from those of the other?

3. How did the fight to defend Scripture's accuracy distort the effort to discover Scripture's meaning?

Long

1. Compare and contrast the schools of Alexandria and Antioch and their different approaches to biblical interpretation. What is the concept of *theoria*, as developed in the school of Antioch? How does it help the interpreter to apply a biblical text?

Quiz

1. (T/F) The school of Alexandria was known for its allegorical approach to the interpretation of Scripture.

2. (T/F) The school of Antioch was known for its literal approach to the interpretation of Scripture.

3. (T/F) In his "redemptive-movement hermeneutic," William Webb called for evangelicals to move beyond what Scripture teaches and develop an ultimate ethic for contemporary culture.

4. (T/F) As a result of his "scientific" approach to the interpretation of Scripture, Charles Hodge denied the historicity of the Old Testament book of Genesis.

5. (T/F) Robert Bellarmine, one of Protestantism's post-Reformation apologists, argued against the Roman Catholic Church's claim to sole authority in terms of interpreting Scripture.

6. _____ was an early church father who championed biblical interpretation that focused on the intention of Scripture. He focused on a literal interpretation of Scripture and emphasized the need to determine the meaning of the author. His principle would become a major theme in the Reformation and in modern hermeneutics.
   a) Gregory the Great
   b) Jerome
   c) Augustine
   d) Clement of Alexandria

7. As one of the most influential medieval interpreters, _____ emphasized the literal sense of Scripture and was known for what was called the "double-literal sense" of Scripture. According to this view, he maintained a value for the Old Testament writings (and their literal significance) in and of themselves while also focusing on their ultimate value in pointing toward Christ.
   a) Andrew of St. Victor
   b) Hugh of St. Victor
   c) Origen
   d) Nicholas of Lyra

8. _____ was a post-Reformer who hoped to inspire renewal among the churches. He sought to introduce people to Scripture in ways other than through sermons. Some of his suggestions included fathers leading their families in Bible studies, personal reading of Scripture, public reading of Scripture during worship, and small group Bible studies.

a) William Pope
b) John Owen
c) Hugh of St. Victor
d) Philipp Jakob Spener

9. Martin Luther and John Calvin both agreed that familiarity with the book of _____ was a key element to properly interpreting the Bible.

a) Romans
b) Galatians
c) Genesis
d) Revelation

10. In response to the critical method, _____ argued for a mediating position between two extremes. He pointed out that evangelicals tend to respond to critical methods in one of two ways: either they abandon their faith altogether or they resort to fundamentalism. He suggested, rather, that evangelicals should welcome critical methods while denying that they would do away with biblical authority.

a) E. D. Hirsch
b) Hans Frei
c) Alister McGrath
d) Kevin Vanhoozer

ANSWER KEY

1. T, 2. T, 3. T, 4. F, 5. F, 6. B, 7. D, 8. D, 9. A, 10. C

CHAPTER 9

The Existence and Knowledge of God

You Should Know

- Throughout its history, the church has believed in God's existence and that his existence can be demonstrated and perhaps even proven.

- The early church argued for the existence of God both from general and special revelation. There was disagreement as to the expressibility and the knowability of God.

- During the Middle Ages both Anselm and Thomas Aquinas proved to be highly influential thinkers regarding their proofs for the existence of God. Anselm's ontological argument and Aquinas's cosmological and teleological arguments for the existence of God have shaped much of the church's history concerning arguments for God's existence.

- During the Reformation both Martin Luther and John Calvin worked to make strong distinctions between the efficaciousness of general and special revelation. While general revelation should lead man to an accurate knowledge of God, only special revelation is capable of accomplishing this.

- Numerous changes have occurred in the modern period. Some have questioned and even rejected the existence and knowability of God. Traditional arguments have been set aside and prominent atheist thinkers have promulgated their thinking. Still, other Christian apologists have risen to the occasion and have offered their own well-reasoned defenses.

- The ontological argument for the existence of God is an *a priori* argument which suggests that "God is that being than which nothing greater can be conceived."

- The teleological argument for the existence of God is an *a posteriori* argument for the existence of God, which is based on the experience of purpose or design in the universe. God is said to be this designer who directs all natural things to their appointed and purposeful end.

- The cosmological argument for the existence of God is an *a posteriori* argument which moves from some experience in the cosmos, or world — motion, efficient causes, beings that possess contingent or possible existence, and the hierarchy of being — and concluding with the existence of God.

- C. S. Lewis revived the moral argument for the existence of God. By moving from the fact of human quarrels and the moral law that these presuppose, to the reality of God as the moral Lawgiver whose law people break, he set forth a foundation not only for the existence of God, but for the message of Christians: "They tell you how the demands of this law, which you and I cannot meet, have been met on our behalf, how God himself becomes a man to save man from the disapproval of God."

Essay Questions

Short

1. In what ways is Luther's distinction between God as hidden and revealed similar to Calvin's distinction between God as Creator and God as redeemer? In what ways is it different?

2. Calvin argued that our knowledge of God has three sources. What are they and why was Calvin ultimately pessimistic about the ability of humans to make good use of them?

3. How do modern versions of the cosmological argument from Paley and Craig differ from the classic statement made by Aquinas?

Long

1. Summarize in your own words the ontological argument for God's existence. What is the difference between Aquinas's cosmological argument and his teleological argument for God's existence? Summarize them in your own words.

Quiz

1. (T/F) Alvin Plantinga argued that belief in God is a properly basic belief, meaning that belief in God is rational to accept without accepting it on the basis of any other propositions or beliefs at all.

2. (T/F) Immanuel Kant rejected the traditional *moral* argument for the existence of God but articulated his own versions of the *ontological*, *cosmological*, and *teleological* arguments in support of the existence of God.

3. (T/F) The apophatic tradition used a negative approach when speaking of the inexpressibility of God. This approach sought to express what and who God is not.

4. (T/F) An innate sense of God's existence is an example of special revelation.

5. (T/F) The incarnation of Christ is an example of special revelation.

6. _____ reworked the cosmological argument for the existence of God, arguing that the universe had a beginning. To prove this, who pointed to the "big bang" theory and the second law of thermodynamics?
   a) Sam Harris
   b) C. S. Lewis
   c) William Craig
   d) Alvin Plantinga

7. _____ sought to apply the principles of logical positivism to statements about God's existence. Because he could not verify anything supernatural such as God's existence through his senses, he concluded that God's existence is logically misguided.

a) Norman Malcolm
b) C. S. Lewis
c) Alvin Plantinga
d) Frederick Ferre

8. In opposition to the apophatic tradition of man's inability to know God and to express knowledge about him, _____ presented a more positive perspective. Because God has left remnants of himself in the created order, he believed man was able to know something of God. He further argued for a more introspective approach to knowing God as the believer is to enter into oneself in order to go down a mystical path to God.

a) Bonaventure
b) John Calvin
c) Thomas Aquinas
d) Thomas à Kempis

9. _____ argued not only for the existence of God but also for the existence of a triune God by speaking of love. The fact that humans, as image bearers, love other humans points to the Trinity, since love must include the one who loves, the one who is loved, and love itself.

a) William Paley
b) Kevin Vanhoozer
c) Augustine
d) David Hume

10. _____ attacked the teleological argument for the existence of God. He also argued against the existence of God using evidence from evil, suggesting that if God is both all-powerful and good then evil should not exist. Since evil does exist, then he concluded that either evil is good or that God does not exist.

a) Stephen Charnock
b) William Paley
c) David Hume
d) Hans Frei

ANSWER KEY

1. T, 2. F, 3. T, 4. F, 5. T, 6. C, 7. A, 8. D, 9. C, 10. C

CHAPTER 10

The Character of God

You Should Know

- The church, throughout its history, has studied the characteristics of God in order to comprehend who God is and what he is like.

- Augustine believed that God's attributes are not added to his essence but are true of the totality of his essence.

- While some in the early church spoke of God's attributes in detail, others took more of an apophatic approach and spoke of what *cannot be said* of God rather than positively affirming God's attributes.

- Thomas Aquinas made an important contribution to the discussion of God's attributes when he distinguished between God's attributes that are shared to some degree with humans and those attributes that are unique to God alone.

- Both the Lutherans and the Calvinists opposed the Socinians who denied that God had the knowledge of future contingencies. The Socinians' endeavor to preserve man's libertarian free will meant that not even God would have the ability to influence human decisions and the actions that would accord to God's plan and purpose.

- In keeping with the usual critical spirit of the time, theologians of the modern period launched attacks against the traditional formulation of the doctrine of God.

- Addressing the topic of God's "repentance" and unchangeableness, John Calvin spoke of Scripture's use of anthropomorphisms.

- Middle knowledge is the knowledge God possesses of all things that can take place involving an act of human will before God freely chooses to decree something about them.

- Friedrich Schleiermacher opposed the church's historical approach to listing and defining God's attributes; he instead sought to reformulate the Christian faith in terms of a self-conscious feeling of dependence on God.

- Arguing against the traditional notion of a perfect, immutable, static, impassible, and transcendent God, Alfred North Whitehead and Charles Hartshorne both contributed to what has become known as process theology.

Essay Questions

Short

1. How does Augustine help Christians to understand how the various attributes of God are related to each other?

2. What role does the theory of accommodation play in Calvin's account of the divine attributes?

3. What was the concrete effect of process theology's distinction between God's primordial nature (or abstract essence) and his consequent nature (or concrete actuality)?

Long

1. Explain divine foreknowledge and human freedom, and the theological problem between the two. How does middle knowledge attempt to solve this theological problem of the relationship between divine foreknowledge and human freedom?

Quiz

1. (T/F) Philosophy has had a large impact on the way the church has understood God's attributes.

2. (T/F) The early church writers are known for detailing God's attributes in a systematic way.

3. (T/F) While Lutheran theologians generally affirmed the reality of middle knowledge, Reformed theologians typically rejected it.

4. (T/F) The doctrine of God's attributes was a significant point of disagreement between Protestants and Roman Catholics.

5. (T/F) Rooting his thinking in the self-giving nature of the triune God, Karl Barth focused on God as being the one who loves in freedom and gives himself to human beings.

6. The early church believed in God's impassibility, which became the basis for the early church's rejection of the heresy of _____.

   a) Nestorianism
   b) Pelagianism
   c) Arianism
   d) Patripassianism

7. The _____ tradition used a negative approach when speaking of the inexpressibility of God. This approach sought to express what and who God is not.

   a) Aliphatic
   b) Apophatic
   c) Kataphatic
   d) Negaphatic

8. _____ made an important contribution to the discussion of God's attributes when he distinguished between God's attributes that are shared to some degree with humans and those attributes that are unique to God alone.

   a) Thomas Aquinas
   b) Anselm
   c) Origen
   d) Augustine

9. _____ sought to harmonize human freedom with God's foreknowledge and predestination by appealing to what he called middle knowledge.

   a) Luis de Molina
   b) John Calvin

c) Thomas Aquinas
d) Thomas à Kempis

10. _____ opposed the Socinians and argued that God can know contingent events and decisions because God's decree determines the decisions and events that must and will take place.

a) John Sanders
b) Origen
c) Friedrich Schleiermacher
d) Francis Turretin

ANSWER KEY

1. T, 2. F, 3. T, 4. F, 5. T, 6. D, 7. B, 8. A, 9. A, 10. D

CHAPTER 11

God in Three Persons: The Trinity

You Should Know

- Distinguishing itself from all other religions, Christianity has historically believed that God eternally exists as three persons, Father, Son, and Holy Spirit; each person is fully God, and there is one God.

- Augustine articulated what would later be called the "double procession" of the Spirit, meaning that the Spirit proceeds from both the Father and the Son.

- At the Third Council of Toledo in 589, a one-word alteration was made to the historical Nicene Creed. This word — *filioque* ("and the Son") — was inserted into the creed to speak of the procession of the Spirit from the Father "and the Son."

- In defending the traditional view of the Trinity against heretics, John Calvin used the novel term *autotheos* (God of himself) to express the deity of the Son and the Spirit. That is, both the Son, and thus the Spirit, is "God of himself," and does not derive his deity from the Father. He, thus, denied the notion that the Father infused the other persons with deity.

- Because the modern period has been characterized by a rise of materialism, agnosticism, and atheism, the doctrine of the Trinity has been de-emphasized. What has historically been considered a cardinal doctrine of the faith has come to be relegated to something of little importance.

- The economic Trinity refers to the different roles and activities of the three persons in relationship to the world.

- Monarchianism was an early church heresy that emphasized the oneness of God to the detriment of the plurality of the persons.

- Tertullian was the early church father known for developing the clearest doctrine of the Trinity that had been formulated up to his time. His articulation of the Trinity would become the foundation for the church's definition of the Trinity.

- Known for his defense of the Creed of Nicea against Arianism, Athanasius defended the notion that "the fullness of the Father's Godhead is the being of the Son, and the Son is whole God." Therefore, whatever the Father is, so is the Son. He believed this to be true with one exception — the Son is not the Father.

- The teaching of "Oneness" Pentecostals is a contemporary example of the heresy of modalism.

Essay Questions

Short

1. What conceptual and linguistic distinction did Tertullian make that influenced all further work on the doctrine of the Trinity?

2. What is the "ontological Trinity" as opposed to the "economic Trinity"?

3. Why is Barth's theology of the Trinity called the "social Trinity"?

Long

1. Summarize how the Cappadocian Fathers expressed the unity and difference among the persons of the Trinity. What terms did they use?

Quiz

1. (T/F) According to the early church notion of a "Trinitarian" consciousness, baptisms were rendered incomplete unless the candidate was baptized in the name of the Trinity.

2. (T/F) Thomas Aquinas believed that it is possible to attain the knowledge of the Trinity by the use of one's natural reason.

3. (T/F) The Reformers denounced the teaching of Faustus Socinus as anti-Trinitarian and dangerous.

4. (T/F) Karl Barth considered the doctrine of the Trinity to be essential to a right understanding of Christian doctrine.

5. The early church received its monotheism from _____.
   a) Aristotelian philosophy
   b) Greek mythology
   c) Judaism
   d) Islam

6. _____ was an early church heresy that understood Jesus to be nothing more than an ordinary man who happened to be unusually good and holy.
   a) Modalistic monarchianism
   b) Dynamic monarchianism
   c) Arianism
   d) Nestorianism

7. _____ was an early church heresy that taught that there is one God who can be designated by three different names (Father, Son, and Holy Spirit) at different times, though these three were not considered distinct persons but rather different modes of the one God.
   a) Arianism
   b) Dynamic monarchianism
   c) Eutychianism
   d) Modalistic monarchianism

8. Developed by Origen, the notion of the _____ Trinity referred to the eternal and ordered relationships that exist between the persons of the Trinity.
   a) Ontological
   b) Immanent
   c) Economic
   d) Dynamic

God in Three Persons: The Trinity | 49

9. The Cappadocian fathers — Basil the Great, Gregory of Nyssa, and _____ — are known for their formulation and defense of the doctrine of the Trinity.

    a) Clement of Alexandria
    b) Gregory Nazianzus
    c) Bernard of Clairvaux
    d) Athanasius

10. At the Council of _____, the early church reworked the Nicene Creed to produce the Nicene-Constantinopolitan Creed, which served to produce a clear affirmation of the deity of the Son and the Spirit.

    a) Constantinople
    b) Ephesus
    c) Chalcedon
    d) Nicaea

ANSWER KEY

1. T, 2. F, 3. T, 4. T, 5. C, 6. B, 7. D, 8. A, 9. B, 10. A

CHAPTER 12

Creation

You Should Know

- The church has historically understood God to have created the cosmos *ex nihilo* (out of nothing) in the recent past, possibly five to six thousand years ago.

- The early church had to confront ideas of evolution long before Charles Darwin came to be. Ancient philosophies opposed the notion of a Creator.

- Medieval scholastic theologians — such as Anselm — sought to prove creation *ex nihilo* by reason alone, without an appeal to Scripture. John Driedo, on the other hand, argued from Scripture, saying that the Bible indicated that the creation of the universe had occurred about four thousand years before the coming of Christ.

- Martin Luther, during the Reformation, argued that the universe was not over six thousand years old and that it was created *ex nihilo*.

- John Calvin believed that the universe would remain in existence for a total of about six thousand years and that the universe was about five thousand years old during his time.

- Six prominent approaches toward interpreting the biblical record of creation became important among evangelicals, including the framework hypothesis, the gap theory, the day-age theory, the intermittent-day theory, the fully-gifted creation theory, and the literal approach. This literal approach — also called "young earth creationism" or "scientific creationism" — associated itself with the historical viewpoint of the church. In doing so, it understood the other approaches to be compromises with scientific findings, which were suspect at best.

- Augustine addressed the popular speculations of the time that sought to determine what God was doing before he created. He suggested that God created time when he created the universe. As a result, time did not exist before creation.

- The Intelligent Design movement set out to attack naturalism and to establish the fact that God's work in the world can be empirically detected.

Essay Questions

Short

1. How did Augustine interpret the days of Genesis 1?

2. How did La Peyrère's ideas anticipate the controversies over creation and the interpretation of Genesis that would come to characterize the modern period?

3. What challenges from geology preceded the publication of Darwin's *On the Origin of Species* (1850), and in what ways did theologians attempt to respond to them? What specifically about Darwin's theories challenged the biblical account of creation?

Long

1. Summarize and explain both young earth creationism and intelligent design. How are they similar to one another; how are they different?

Quiz

1. (T/F) B. B. Warfield attempted to find common ground between biblical creation and evolutionary theory. He affirmed that there is no conflict between holding a nuanced theory of evolution and also being a Christian.

2. (T/F) The church has historically understood God to have created the cosmos *ex nihilo* in the recent past.

3. (T/F) The "gap theory" is considered the historical viewpoint of the church concerning the creation of the universe.

4. (T/F) Martin Luther agreed with Augustine regarding his understanding of the six days of creation.

5. (T/F) The ninth century marked the beginning of attacks launched against the historical position of divine creation.

6. _____ provided a unique theory of divine creation. He believed Moses to be referring to an invisible spiritual world in Genesis 1:1, not the actual visible heaven and earth in which material mankind lives. Accordingly, the visible heaven and earth were not created until after the fall of the rational creatures that made up the original spiritual world. This view never caught on in the early church.

   a) Irenaeus
   b) Origen
   c) Justin Martyr
   d) Polycarp

7. _____ introduced a new allegorical or nonliteral way of interpreting the biblical account in Genesis 1. He understood the six days not to be literal days. Instead, he understood the "days" of creation as progressive knowledge of divine creation, but they did not refer to actual days of creation. He believed that creation took place in one day. Even with his nonliteral interpretation, he still believed that the universe was relatively young and that a view of an old earth should be rejected.

   a) Augustine
   b) Thomas Aquinas
   c) John Calvin
   d) Wayne Grudem

8. _____ made the bold calculated assertion that the precise date of God's creation of the universe was October 23, 4004 BC.

a) Martin Luther
b) Isaac La Peyrère
c) James Ussher
d) Francis Turretin

9. _____ presented his theory of catastrophism, which maintained that the geological history of the earth could be attributed to a number of catastrophic floods. This view accounted for numerous floods that preceded the Noachian flood. Thus, this view served to reduce the geological significance of the flood of Noah's time and further expanded earth history well beyond the traditional biblical view.

a) Georges Cuvier
b) James Ussher
c) Isaac La Peyrère
d) Charles Lyell

10. _____ popularized another theory called uniformitarianism, which explained away the Noachian flood by reducing it to a geological nonevent. The whole rock record was said to be explained by slow gradual processes, which included localized catastrophes like volcanoes and earthquakes.

a) Georges Cuvier
b) James Ussher
c) Isaac La Peyrère
d) Charles Lyell

ANSWER KEY
1. T, 2. T, 3. F, 4. F, 5. F, 6. B, 7. A, 8. C, 9. A, 10. D

CHAPTER 13

Providence

You Should Know

- The church has historically believed that God exercises complete control over his creation through his providence.

- While the early church affirmed God's meticulous providence, it also sought to affirm human free will. The early church affirmed the compatibility of human freedom and divine providence.

- In response to the problem of evil, some admitted that man simply cannot speculate and know why God permits evil. Others sought to offer solutions to the problem.

- Augustine argued that evil is not something that exists. Instead, "evil is nothing but a privation of good."

- According to Thomas Aquinas, evil occurs when a thing fails in goodness. God is said to be the ultimate reason for evil's existence. This is true in that he created a world where things can and do fall away from original goodness. Nevertheless, God is not the cause of this falling away.

- That Erasmus would suggest that human free will would cooperate at all with divine grace in obtaining salvation was, according to Martin Luther, more devaluing of divine grace than Pelagianism. Luther, in the end, gave no place for human free will in salvation.

- Jonathan Edwards rejected the idea that the phrase "the author of sin" could mean that God is the agent, actor, or doer of any wicked thing. Such an idea would be blasphemous. However, if "the author of sin" refers to God as the "permitter" of sin as a part of a larger plan that brings about holy and most excellent ends and purposes, then Edwards was agreeable to the phrase.

- During the Reformation, Martin Luther, in his *The Bondage of the Will*, opposed Erasmus and his work, *Freedom of the Will*, concerning the issue of human freedom.

- Rejecting both the notions of "hard" determinism and "soft" determinism, Jacob Arminius believed there to be a contradiction between human freedom and any kind of causation.

- During the modern period, deism proved to be a popular worldview that exchanged God's personal providence for an impersonal mechanistic model. In this view, God was thought to essentially wind up the universe like a wristwatch and let it go.

Essay Questions

Short

1. How does Augustine deal with the problem of evil? How does Aquinas use his theory of causation to explain the relationship between God's providence and human free will?

2. What was Calvin's doctrine of providence? How did he define it, apply it, and protect it from misuse?

3. What is a theodicy, and what is the basic pattern most theodicies take when attempting to deal with the problem of evil?

Long

1. What is the free will defense? Summarize and explain how it was used by Tertullian, Origen, and Augustine.

Quiz

1. (T/F) The early church believed evil to be something that comes as a result of God's *permission* rather than from his *willing*.

2. (T/F) While the early church affirmed God's meticulous providence, it scoffed at the notion of human free will.

3. (T/F) Origen was ridiculed for teaching what came to be understood as a fatalistic doctrine of human free will.

4. (T/F) Martin Luther believed Erasmus' teachings to be more dangerous than those of Pelagius regarding the freedom of the human will.

5. (T/F) Lutherans suggested that divine foreknowledge is not dependent on the divine decrees, while Reformed theologians associated providence with the divine decrees.

6. _____ argued that evil is not something that exists. Instead, "evil is nothing but a privation of good." Everything was created good, but humans can fall away from this goodness through an abuse of their free will. Yet, he affirmed that God decreed the abuse of Adam and Eve's free will and thus the fall of mankind into sin and death.

   a) Irenaeus
   b) Thomas Aquinas
   c) Augustine
   d) Athanasius

7. _____ believed that nothing takes place in the world apart from divine deliberation.

   a) John Cassian
   b) John Calvin
   c) Pelagius
   d) Jacob Arminius

8. _____ presented a "risk" model that maintains that the divine goal for creation is fixed but that the means to its realization are flexible. God, thus, does not foreordain the future but rather grants humans libertarian freedom to choose as they will without any divine causation.

   a) John Sanders
   b) Bruce Ware
   c) Karl Barth
   d) Kevin Vanhoozer

9. _____ appealed to Aristotelian thought in his discussion of providence, especially as it concerns the idea of agents acting toward an end or goal. God is said to be the first and causal agent who directs everything to accomplish his purpose. God not only exercises immediate control over everything. He also uses secondary means to accomplish his rule over the universe. God's foreknowledge functioned to prepare some things of necessity such that they happen of necessity.

   a) Basil the Great
   b) Thomas Aquinas
   c) Gregory of Nyssa
   d) Gregory of Nazianzus

10. _____ hijacked the doctrine of providence, forcing it into his reformulation of the Christian faith as the feeling of absolute dependence on the divine spirit of the world. Divine government is working toward the perfection of the human spirit in unity with this divine spirit through Christ. Thus, there is only one unified goal for everything that exists, and everything that exists must be considered in relation to that unified goal.

   a) Wolfhart Pannenberg
   b) Jacob Arminius
   c) Friedrich Schleiermacher
   d) Karl Barth

ANSWER KEY

1. T, 2. F, 3. F, 4. T, 5. T, 6. C, 7. B, 8. A, 9. B, 10. C

CHAPTER 14

Angels, Satan, and Demons

You Should Know

- The church has historically believed in the existence of another sphere of reality beyond the material realm and the visible world of human beings, one inhabited by angels and demons.

- Dionysius the Pseudo-Areopagite made the greatest contribution to the early church's beliefs concerning the doctrine of angels. His elaborate and detailed description of angelic beings had a significant influence over key church leaders in the following centuries.

- Many think of the works of Thomas Aquinas when they consider the medieval church's teaching on angels and demons. While his influence was significant, and even earned him the title "Angelic Doctor," many others contributed to this doctrine as well.

- Besides the Word of God and prayer, Martin Luther believed that spiritual warfare was the third key to the spiritual theologian.

- Two primary developments concerning the doctrine of angels, Satan, and demons occurred during the modern period. First, liberal Christianity demonstrated a bias against all things supernatural and, thus, neglected the doctrine. Second, more conservative Christians reacted to the liberals by relegating the doctrine to a position of periphery.

- In his *The City of God*, Augustine differentiated between two types of angelic beings, the angels of God and the angels of the devil.

- During the early church, Augustine taught that the number of fallen angels would be replaced by an equal amount of human Christians.

- In his *Sentences*, Peter Lombard secured a place for the study of angels within academic theology; from the time of his writing on, the doctrine of angels would be studied as a part of the theological curriculum for anyone preparing for ministry.

- John Calvin doubted the existence of guardian angels, due to the lack of scriptural support.

Essay Questions

Short

1. How did Aquinas describe the nature of angels?

2. How does Luther counsel Christians to respond to attacks from the devil?

3. How does Barth differ from the traditional explanation of the origin of demons?

Long

1. Summarize some of the activities the early church ascribed to angels. Now, consider specifically how Origen and Augustine addressed the subject: What were the functions of guardian angels according to Origen? In Augustine's theology, how is the redemption of humanity related to the fall of angels, specifically with regard to their numerical extent?

Quiz

1. (T/F) The doctrines of angels, Satan, and demons have never been a source of extreme contention in churches.

2. (T/F) The early church believed that angels had the power to reveal themselves physically, taking on the form and likeness of humans.

3. (T/F) Origen and Cyprian taught that both believers and unbelievers may experience demon possession.

4. (T/F) Thomas Aquinas taught the reality of personal guardian angels that have been assigned to specific individuals for the purpose of protection and safety in the presence of evil angels.

5. (T/F) Thomas Aquinas rejected the notion that one-third of all angels fell along with Satan after his rebellion against God.

6. _____ believed in the salvation of angels, that fallen angels could be restored to their original position.

   a) Origen
   b) Tertullian
   c) Irenaeus
   d) Clement of Alexandria

7. _____ made the greatest contribution to the early church's beliefs concerning the doctrine of angels. His elaborate and detailed description of the angelic beings had a significant influence over key church leaders in the following centuries.

   a) John Cassian
   b) Gregory Thaumaturgus
   c) Dionysius the Pseudo-Areopagite
   d) Polycarp

8. _____ essentially denied the existence of angels and assumed that Christ's and the apostle's speech concerning angels were uttered without any real conviction that such beings actually exist. He relegated this doctrine to a position of childish beliefs. He even dismissed the biblical affirmations of the existence of Satan and his demons. Nevertheless, he affirmed the positive that can come from believing in and teaching on the devil, since it makes clear the reality of godlessness.

   a) Billy Graham
   b) Thomas Aquinas
   c) Karl Barth
   d) Friedrich Schleiermacher

9. _____ was known for engaging in intense spiritual warfare during the early church. He opposed demonic influences through an

ascetic lifestyle, which would serve to promote asceticism as a whole in the early church as an antidote against demons.

   a) Origen
   b) Clement of Alexandria
   c) Antony
   d) Athenagoras

10. _____ was responsible for the resurgence of interest in the doctrine of angels during the twentieth century. He opposed many conservatives who had simply neglected the doctrine; he further was opposed to mere speculation on the matter.

   a) David Strauss
   b) Kevin Vanhoozer
   c) C. S. Lewis
   d) Karl Barth

ANSWER KEY

1. T, 2. T, 3. F, 4. T, 5. F, 6. A, 7. C, 8. D, 9. C, 10. D

CHAPTER 15

The Creation and Nature of Humanity

You Should Know

- Following the apostolic era, the early church affirmed the complexity of human nature, the dignity of human beings as creatures made in the image of God, and spoke of the immortality of humanity.

- The medieval era was characterized by an emphasis on monasticism and asceticism. In keeping with previous dualistic approaches to human nature, ascetics understood the body and all things material to be inherently evil. This negative perception of the body impacted numerous other areas of theology.

- John Calvin believed man to be originally created in the divine image. While Calvin did not limit the divine image to the inner being of the human, he did tend to emphasize the mind and heart over the material. The method he used to determine the image of God had to do with what he observed to be restored in the human in salvation.

- In keeping with the common negative attitude toward traditional doctrine, theologians in the modern era doubted the truth of Scripture and thus the church's traditional teaching on human nature. Part of the shift away from traditional teaching came as a result of "secular" disciplines such as psychology, sociology, and anthropology. These disciplines, with their nonbiblical, antisupernaturalistic, evolutionary, and empirical methods, presented a stalwart challenge to traditional doctrine.

- Four primary theologians during the early church were most significant in their contributions to the development of the doctrine of humanity: Irenaeus, Tertullian, Origen, and Augustine.

- Tertullian proposed an original idea called traducianism, which suggests that both the soul and body come into existence through the act of intercourse.

- Origen offered an original view concerning the origin of the soul. He suggested that because God is omnipotent, God must always have a world over which he can exercise his power. Thus, there must be an invisible spiritual world comprised of rational creatures who all abused their free will. As a result of this abuse, the actual visible world became the new home of the fallen creatures. Those who had fallen the least became angels; those who had fallen the most became demons; and those who had fallen an intermediate degree became humans.

- Thomas Aquinas spoke of a threefold image of creation, re-creation, and likeness: the first is present in all men, the second only in Christians, and the third only in those who are in heaven.

- Karl Barth rejected the historicity of the biblical account of Adam and Eve; thus, he rejected the traditional perspective on the *imago Dei*. Rather than focusing on who man is or what he does, he believed the image of God had to do with relationality, first within the members of the Trinity, then between God and man, and finally between man and man. Humans reflect this image and plurality of persons primarily as male relates to female and female relates to male.

Essay Questions

Short

1. In what ways did the church resist the influence of Plato on its anthropology? In what ways was it too susceptible to the influence of Plato?

2. Why can Luther's position be described as a holistic dualism, despite his talk of body, soul, and spirit?

3. What social and intellectual challenges have led contemporary theologians to revise the doctrine of humanity?

Long

1. According to the early church, what were the basic elements of the image of God in humanity, and what was the main inspiration for this understanding? Where did Aquinas locate the image of God and how did he distinguish this from the likeness of God? What results did this have for his understanding of the human person and its constituent parts?

Quiz

1. (T/F) The early church writers spoke of human nature as consisting of multiple parts.

2. (T/F) Tertullian was a trichotomist.

3. (T/F) Augustine was a strong advocate of the dichotomist position and believed the Bible to present a clear and convincing case for the position.

4. (T/F) Regarding the origin of the soul, Martin Luther was a traducianist.

5. (T/F) Lutheran and Reformed post-Reformation theologians embraced dichotomy.

6. _____ is credited with originating the trichotomist perspective.
   a) Origen
   b) Tertullian
   c) Irenaeus
   d) Clement of Alexandria

7. The _____ view of the origin of the soul suggests that the soul is not conceived at the point of conception in the womb but rather is infused from outside the infant before his complete vitality but after childbirth.

a) Creationist
b) Functionalist
c) Existentialist
d) Traducianist

8. _____ made a distinction between the image and the likeness of God; he associated the immaterial aspects of the human with the divine image, and the material aspects to the likeness of God.

a) Cyprian
b) Tatian
c) Thomas Aquinas
d) Julius Africanus

9. _____ proposed a two-fold concept of the image of God. Before the fall, the image of God consisted of both natural gifts (understanding and integrity of heart) and supernatural gifts (faith, love, holiness, and righteousness). Due to the fall, humankind totally lost its supernatural gifts, while its natural gifts are devastated. Through the renewal of the Spirit in salvation, the whole image is gradually restored, though complete restoration awaits the future glorification.

a) Augustine
b) Victorinus
c) John Calvin
d) Huldrych Zwingli

10. _____ opposed the adoption of any singular approach to understanding the divine image over another. Instead, he proposed a holistic approach. He pointed to Scripture's emphasis on the whole man as the image of God. He, thus, did not emphasize one part of man as independent from other parts. In the end, it is illegitimate to consider human nature as divided into higher and lower parts.

a) Emil Brunner
b) C. S. Lewis
c) Gerhard von Rad
d) G. C. Berkouwer

ANSWER KEY

1. T, 2. F, 3. F, 4. T, 5. T, 6. C, 7. A, 8. C, 9. C, 10. D

CHAPTER 16

Sin

You Should Know

- The church has historically believed that God's plan of salvation through Jesus Christ is a response to and is made necessary because of human sin.

- Cyprian taught that infant baptism was necessary to renew infants from their original filth. For Cyprian, baptism is necessary for infants not because of any personal sin, but because they have inherited sin and death from Adam.

- According to Pelagius, God's grace is always an external aid to man, since man has no internal tendency to sin. Man is not inclined toward evil. In fact, he does not inherit Adam's sin at all. Instead, Adam's sin leaves a bad example for humans but does not incline them to sin. Thus, believers are able to live without sin.

- Chief among those who reacted against the heresy of Pelagianism was Augustine.

- John Cassian agreed with Pelagius that human will is free to choose good or evil; yet, he agreed with Augustine in his insistence that God's grace works to assist the will. According to Cassian, the will is always good enough to cooperate with God's grace. Thus, the will plays a part in overcoming sin.

- Thomas Aquinas introduced a distinction between mortal and venial sins. The one who sins by turning away from the greatest goal — God — is guilty of mortal sin and deserves eternal punishment. The one who sins without turning away from God is guilty of venial sin but can be forgiven, and he is not deserving of eternal damnation.

- John Wesley suggested that prevenient grace is given to all mankind, which serves to remove one's disabilities due to a corrupt human nature. This removal of the effects of original sin through prevenient grace enables all people to pursue salvation.

- At the Council of Trent, the Roman Catholic Church denied Luther's and Calvin's doctrines of total depravity and total inability. Instead, Rome believed man to retain some ability to cooperate with God's grace in salvation.

- Jacob Arminius believed original sin to affect all people; he further embraced the doctrine of total inability. Yet, Arminianism proposed the notion of prevenient grace, which was said to be a grace given to man to remove the negative effects of original sin.

Essay Questions

Short

1. How did Calvin modify Augustine's understanding of the transmission of original sin? What did Calvin mean by total depravity and total inability?

2. On what main point of anthropology did the Council of Trent disagree with the Reformers?

3. What is the role of prevenient grace in the theologies of Arminius and Wesley?

Long

1. Summarize the way Pelagius relates the sin of Adam to the condition of humanity and contrast this with Augustine's view of the same issue. How does Augustine describe the situation of Adam both before and after the fall?

Quiz

1. (T/F) Martin Luther believed the human will to be enslaved to sin and corruption.

2. (T/F) Charles Hodge argued for a realist view of the imputation of Adam's sin to explain the relationship between Adam's sin and humanity.

3. (T/F) Clement of Alexandria taught that Adam's sin affected him only and was not transmitted to his descendants.

4. (T/F) John Calvin believed Adam's first sin to be the sin of gluttony.

5. (T/F) John Wesley believed in total depravity.

6. In seeking to explain the fall of the human race, _____ began by speaking of Adam in an original neutral state. Man was created neither mortal nor immortal but was capable of being both. The choice was Adam's. If Adam had chosen the things of immortality, he would have become God. If, on the other hand, Adam had chosen the things of death, man would bring about death on himself. Of course, Adam chose death, and death was his reward. Thus, the blame for sin was placed on Adam and not God.

   a) Theophilus
   b) Chrysostom
   c) Irenaeus
   d) Theodoret

7. Known as the father of the social gospel, _____ approached sin more as a social phenomenon than an individual problem.

   a) Gustavo Gutiérrez
   b) Alvin Plantinga
   c) Walter Rauschenbusch
   d) Immanuel Kant

8. For _____, infant baptism was necessary to renew an infant from its original filth. Baptism is necessary for infants not because of any personal sin, but because they have inherited sin and death from Adam.

   a) Charles Spurgeon
   b) Cyprian
   c) Pelagius
   d) James Petigru Boyce

9. According to _____, the will is always good enough to cooperate with God's grace and is, thus, able to play a part in overcoming sin.

   a) Pelagianism
   b) Calvinism
   c) Augustinianism
   d) Semi-Pelagianism

10. _____ distanced himself from most evangelicals when he embraced a conditional imputation of Adam's guilt for sin; there must be some conscious and voluntary decision on man's part in approving of a corrupt nature.

   a) Millard Erickson
   b) Herman Bavinck
   c) Charles Hodge
   d) Wayne Grudem

ANSWER KEY

1. T, 2. F, 3. T, 4. T, 5. T, 6. A, 7. C, 8. B, 9. D, 10. A

CHAPTER 17

The Person of Jesus Christ

You Should Know

- The church has historically believed Jesus Christ to be fully God and fully human in one person. It further has believed that he will remain fully God and fully human forever.

- At the fourth ecumenical council, the Council of Chalcedon, the Chalcedonian Creed was composed. There, Eutychianism, Arianism, Apollinarianism, and Nestorianism were all denounced as heresies.

- According to Anselm, in order for Jesus to be able to accomplish salvation, his person could not be a divine nature becoming a human nature, nor a human nature becoming a divine nature, nor two natures simply joining together. Instead, it required one who is both fully divine and fully human.

- A controversy between Martin Luther and Huldrych Zwingli broke out regarding the Lord's Supper. Zwingli accused Luther of Eutychianism, while Zwingli's opponents accused him of Nestorianism.

- Gottfried Thomasius, with his kenotic model, suggested that Christ could not have maintained his full divinity during the incarnation; Christ gave himself over to full human limitation. This self-denial meant that while he did not give up his immanent divine attributes, he did give up his relative divine attributes.

- Thomas Aquinas addressed the church's view on the communication of properties, the question of whether it is proper to speak of Christ's qualities in one nature while referring to his other nature.

He concluded that what is said of either nature may be said of either God or man, since both "God" and "man" refer to the one person of Jesus Christ.

- In his efforts to combat Apollinarianism, Gregory of Nazianzus taught that if Christ only took on part of human nature in his incarnation, he could only redeem that part. If Christ lacked an essential component of human nature, then he was not human. Thus, to say that Christ did not have a soul rendered him something other than a human.

- In a discussion of the traditional title for the Virgin Mary—*theotokos*—Cyril of Alexandria accused Nestorius of believing something that he clearly denied. Nevertheless, Nestorius would be pinned with heresy.

- Docetism: one of the earliest heresies in the church. It denied the full humanity of Jesus and suggested that Jesus simply appeared to be human, though he was only a spirit being.

- Arianism: an early church heresy that affirmed that God could not share his deity with any other being, since to do so would mean that there were two gods. It was further suggested that the eternal and unbegotten God created a Son, Jesus. Jesus was, thus, considered to be a created being and not eternal. Furthermore, it was taught that Jesus does not share the same nature with the Father.

Essay Questions

Short

1. What was Gnosticism's view of matter and how did that view affect its understanding of the incarnation?

2. Why was Luther's understanding of the relationship between Christ's two natures important for his theology of the Eucharist?

3. Explain how Morris defended the traditional understanding of Christ's two natures against the charge that it is incoherent.

Long

1. What decision concerning the nature of Christ was made at the Council of Nicea and ratified at the Council of Constantinople? How did the Council of Chalcedon respond to the heresies of Apollinarianism, Eutychianism (or Monophysitism), Arianism, and Nestorianism? What was its key term for expressing the nature of Christ's person?

Quiz

1. (T/F) The early church believed that the incarnation neither diminished Christ's deity nor elevated his humanity to the level of a superhuman.

2. (T/F) Friedrich Schleiermacher contributed to the undoing of the church's historic consensus on Christology during the modern period. He presented Jesus as an ideal, the one in whom the God-consciousness reached its peak. What set Jesus apart from other men was his absolute dependence on the God-consciousness.

3. (T/F) Only two out of more than three hundred theologians in attendance at the Council of Nicea opposed Arius by signing the creed.

4. (T/F) The Nicene faith of Athanasius would prove victorious over Arianism but would be reversed at the second ecumenical council, the Council of Constantinople.

5. (T/F) While the Reformed tradition denies that the properties of Christ's divine nature have been imparted to his human nature, the Lutheran tradition believes that they have.

6. _____ was an early church heresy that insisted that Jesus was only a man in whom the presence of God was able to work with great power.
   a) Apollinarianism
   b) Ebionism
   c) Eutychianism
   d) Docetism

7. _____ was an early church heresy that believed that in taking on human nature, the Word became united with only a body and not a soul. Jesus' soul was said to be replaced by the divine Word. Thus, Jesus was not an ordinary human being.

   a) Apollinarianism
   b) Ebionism
   c) Eutychianism
   d) Docetism

8. _____ was an early church heresy that combined the two natures of Christ into one different nature. As an example of monophysitism, the heresy taught that Jesus possessed only one nature. It was suggested that Jesus' two natures existed before the incarnation, but they were united in such a way at the incarnation that Jesus only had one remaining nature. Thus, Christ did not share the same nature with humanity.

   a) Apollinarianism
   b) Ebionism
   c) Eutychianism
   d) Nestorianism

9. Docetism was associated with _____ since it drove a wedge between spiritual and physical realities, giving priority to the spiritual.

   a) Eutychianism
   b) Apollinarianism
   c) Arianism
   d) Gnosticism

10. The Council of _____, the fourth ecumenical council, denounced Eutychianism, Arianism, Apollinarianism, and Nestorianism as heresies.

    a) Ephesus
    b) Nicea
    c) Chalcedon
    d) Constantinople

ANSWER KEY

1. T, 2. T, 3. F, 4. F, 5. T, 6. B, 7. A, 8. C, 9. D, 10. C

CHAPTER 18

The Atonement

You Should Know

- Throughout the history of the church, numerous and differing models have been put forward to describe the significance of the atonement.

- The New Testament presents the atoning death of Jesus as a multifaceted diamond in that it accomplishes a number of important things, including expiation, propitiation, redemption, reconciliation, victory over Satan and the demons, an exemplary model, and exchange.

- Irenaeus formulated what would become known as the recapitulation theory, which suggested that Christ repeated the course of human existence in his life with one exception: the sinful life was reversed, and Christ's obedience was exchanged for it. It, however, was not just Christ's life but also his death that brought about the undoing of human sin.

- Origen promoted the "ransom to Satan" theory: the atonement served as a rescue from Satan. According to Origen, Satan had usurped God's rightful ownership of humanity. Christ's death was the ransom payment that would release people from Satan's ownership. Satan was the one who demanded the death of Christ. Nevertheless, Satan did not anticipate the results of the transaction that would take place: once Satan had Christ in his grasp, and had released humanity, he could no longer hold on to Christ.

- Anselm, with his satisfaction theory, believed that it is not right for God to forgive a sin out of mercy alone. Instead, restitution of the honor taken away must be made. Man could not restore this honor by himself; he rightly deserved punishment. But God could be satisfied through one other means: through the sacrifice of Jesus Christ, the God-man.

- The Reformers introduced the penal substitutionary atonement theory. This perspective was similar to Anselm's satisfaction theory, though it differed in that it grounded the atonement in the justice of God rather than the honor of God. Because God is holy, he hates sin and righteously judges it. Thus, a penalty must be paid either by man's punishment or by Christ.

- While the penal substitutionary atonement theory continued to be prominent among Protestants during the modern era, new challenges arose in opposition to it.

- Hugo Grotius proposed the governmental theory of the atonement.

- Peter Abelard developed the moral influence theory of the atonement.

- Friedrich Schleiermacher presented a subjective idea of the atonement by maintaining that Christ redeemed humanity by providing an impeccable example of God-consciousness and dependence on God.

Essay Questions

Short

1. How did Aquinas's contribution to the doctrine of atonement help promote the idea of a salvation that is earned?

2. How does Calvin connect the penal substitution theory to the three offices of Christ?

3. What does Schleiermacher's theory of the atonement have in common with Abelard's theory?

Long

1. Summarize and explain the various views of atonement, showcasing their strengths and weaknesses.

Quiz

1. (T/F) The atonement has never been the subject of discussion in an ecumenical church council.

2. (T/F) The Arminian document, the *Five Articles of the Remonstrants*, was written in response to the Calvinist document, the *Five Articles of Calvinism*.

3. (T/F) Jesus's sufferings were linked to the Passover and to the sacrificial lamb that was offered during the festival.

4. (T/F) The Reformers introduced the penal substitutionary atonement theory.

5. (T/F) In his discussion of the nature of the atonement, Augustine rejected the substitutionary and sacrificial elements as being important to Christ's work.

6. The person most commonly associated with the view that the atonement was rescue from Satan is _____, who popularized the ransom-to-Satan theory of Christ's work.

   a) Tertullian
   b) Athenagoras
   c) Origen
   d) Hippolytus

7. The _____ of the atonement suggests that God, as the ruler of the world, could choose to relax his standards and forgive sinful people in his mercy. As the lawgiver, God himself is not subject to his own law. Instead of simply doing away with the law, God instead relaxes the law. Christ's death met the requirements of this relaxed law. Christ, thus, died not as a satisfaction for the exact penalty, but as a token of God's concern to uphold his moral law.

   a) Recapitulation theory
   b) Governmental theory
   c) Example theory
   d) Moral influence theory

8. Though similar to Anselm's satisfaction theory, the _____ of the atonement differed from the satisfaction theory in that it grounded the atonement in the justice of God rather than the honor of God.

   a) Satisfaction theory
   b) Moral influence theory
   c) Penal substitutionary theory
   d) Recapitulation theory

9. The _____ of the atonement denied that Christ's death was necessary for the payment of sin. Instead, a simple exhibition of God's love is necessary. Christ demonstrated this through his life and death. The death of Christ, therefore, was significant in that it demonstrated God's love for man, though it did not have a necessary connection to the forgiveness of sins.

   a) Satisfaction theory
   b) Moral influence theory
   c) Penal substitutionary theory
   d) Recapitulation theory

10. The _____ of the atonement became the most prominent view for the Protestants during the Reformation.

    a) Governmental theory
    b) Moral influence theory
    c) Christus Victor theory
    d) Penal substitutionary theory

ANSWER KEY

1. T, 2. F, 3. T, 4. T, 5. F, 6. C, 7. B, 8. C, 9. B, 10. D

CHAPTER 19

Resurrection and Ascension

You Should Know

- The church has historically believed that after his crucifixion, Jesus Christ rose on the third day and then ascended into heaven forty days later.

- Celsus, one of the earliest critics of Christianity, enjoyed making fun of the idea of a resurrection. Critics accused the supposed eyewitnesses of wild dreams and fanciful imaginations. Others assumed that the body must have been stolen from the tomb.

- The medieval church continued to affirm the traditional belief concerning these doctrines and even celebrated them on specific days throughout the liturgical year — Good Friday and Easter Sunday.

- Bernard of Clairvaux emphasized the importance of the ascension, claiming that if Christ has risen without ascending then it could not be said that he had "gone through" but only that he had passed away.

- Martin Luther and Huldrych Zwingli differed in their conclusions about the human body of Christ after the ascension. Zwingli concluded that Christ's human body is physically located at the right hand of the Father. As a result, it cannot be physically present during the Lord's Supper. Luther agreed that Christ had physically ascended into heaven, but he disagreed with Zwingli when it came to understanding what it meant to be seated at the right hand of the Father. To Luther, being seated at the right hand of the Father does not refer to a physical place but rather to a position of power.

- As a part of the quest for the historical Jesus, biblical criticism, an attitude of antisupernaturalism, the elevation of reason, and many other factors contributed to the search for the real Jesus in the modern era. This, of course, brought with it challenges to the resurrection and the ascension.

- Rudolph Bultmann emphasized the Christ of faith over the historical Jesus. As a result, he rejected the resurrection and ascension, since they cannot be proven as historical events.

- Wolfhart Pannenberg became the most widely recognized theologian within the twentieth century movement that arose among German theologians who began to defend the historicity of the resurrection of Jesus Christ. He was particularly critical of the well-entrenched view that one's personal encounter with the living Christ becomes the basis for one's certainty about the resurrection of Jesus. Two complementary traditions — one affirming Jesus's appearances after his resurrection, the other recounting the conditions in the tomb after his resurrection (it was empty) — provided the foundation for his insistence on the historicity of the resurrection.

- William Lane Craig distinguished between the resurrection event and its cause, arguing that the event of the resurrection occurs within human history, but the cause of the resurrection is outside human history. The resurrection as event can be verified historically. He noted, however, that the problem comes when one seeks to understand the cause of the resurrection. He pointed out that the best historian could conclude that Jesus rose from the dead, but he could not conclude that God caused Jesus to be raised from the dead. He concluded, however, that a human being may indeed rightly infer from the evidence that God has acted in history.

Essay Questions

Short

1. What are the benefits of Christ's resurrection enumerated by Calvin? What are the benefits of Christ's ascension?

2. What was Bultmann's program of demythologizing the New Testament?

3. On the basis of what complimentary traditions does Pannenberg consider the resurrection to be "very probable"?

Long

1. What objections to the belief in the resurrection came from heretics? From Jews? From pagans? What are some of the reasons why modern critics attacked the doctrine of the resurrection? How did Strauss explain — or explain away — the apostles' witness to the resurrection?

Quiz

1. (T/F) The New Testament writers did not mention any eyewitnesses to the actual resurrection event.

2. (T/F) The church's faith concerning the resurrection and ascension was recorded in the Nicene Creed.

3. (T/F) The medieval church was characterized by its denial of the historical doctrines of the resurrection and ascension of Jesus Christ.

4. (T/F) Both the Lutheran and the Reformed traditions continued to affirm the historic doctrines of the resurrection and ascension of Christ.

5. (T/F) The modern era was characterized by an attitude of anti-supernaturalism, which caused many to doubt the possibility of the resurrection.

6. _____ simply explained the events of the resurrection and ascension away, arguing that the Gospel writers had used mythological language in their writings; thus, these events were not historical events but only mythological ideas.
   a) David Friedrich Strauss
   b) Hermann Samuel Reimarus
   c) Karl Bahrdt
   d) Albert Schweitzer

7. Albert Schweitzer explained the events of the resurrection and ascension away by suggesting that Jesus had a messianic consciousness that was steeped in the eschatological doctrine and expectations of his time.

   a) Karl Barth
   b) Rudolph Bultmann
   c) Karl Bahrdt
   d) Albert Schweitzer

8. _____ emphasized the importance of the ascension, claiming that if Christ has risen without ascending then it could not be said that he had "gone through" but only that he had passed away.

   a) Bernard of Clairvaux
   b) Marcus Minucius Felix
   c) Gregory Thaumaturgus
   d) Origen

9. Martin Luther and _____ came to different conclusions concerning their understanding of the human body of Christ and the nature of his physical location after he had been resurrected and ascended to the right hand of the Father. This disagreement became most pronounced in their debate over the presence of Christ in the Lord's Supper.

   a) Huldrych Zwingli
   b) John Calvin
   c) Erasmus
   d) Philipp Melanchthon

10. _____ popularized the idea that Jesus did not die but rather faked his death and then proclaimed his resurrection.

    a) Faustus Socinus
    b) H. E. G. Paulus
    c) Hugo Grotius
    d) William Paley

ANSWER KEY

1. T, 2. T, 3. F, 4. T, 5. T, 6. A, 7. D, 8. A, 9. A, 10. B

CHAPTER 20

The Holy Spirit

You Should Know

- Throughout the history of the church, little disagreement has existed among Christians concerning the person and work of the Holy Spirit.

- The role of the Spirit in miraculous works became a subject of debate in the early church. An early church movement called Montanism, named after its founder Montanus, incited controversy as its leaders claimed to be the mouthpiece of the Holy Spirit. Their teachings were denounced when it became clear that their words were contrary to truth.

- The error in the heretical movement Arianism had primarily to do with the denial of the deity of Christ. However, it also denied the deity of the Holy Spirit. While the church did not focus on defending the deity of the Holy Spirit to the degree that it defended the deity of Christ, it nevertheless did affirm the deity of the Holy Spirit in the Creed of Nicea.

- To show that the Spirit is not the Son, Augustine affirmed the generation of the Son from the Father and the double procession of the Spirit from both the Father and the Son. Only the Western Church—the Roman Catholic Church and the Protestant churches—affirmed this double procession. The affirmation resulted in the insertion of one word—*filioque* ("and the Son")—into the Latin version of the Nicene Creed. Difference of opinion over this matter would cause a deep division between the Western and the Eastern church. This division continues to this day.

- The East rejected the notion of the Spirit proceeding from two principles or authors. However, the West responded with Augustine saying that the Father and the Son are not two principles but one. Aquinas further argued that the Father and the Son are one in everything and thus together the one source of the Holy Spirit.

- During the Reformation, Martin Luther taught that the Holy Spirit carries out his ministry in believers through the Word of God. Indeed, the Spirit was necessary for understanding God's Word. John Calvin agreed with Luther concerning the relation of the Spirit and God's Word and criticized the Catholic Church for teaching things contrary to God's Word and thus contrary to the Spirit.

- Charles Fox Parham taught that baptism in the Holy Spirit is always accompanied by speaking in tongues. Parham, along with William J. Seymour of the Azusa Street Revival, served to birth Pentecostalism.

- Modalistic monarchianism: the early church heresy that held that there is one God who can be designated by three different names at different times. These were not thought to be three different persons; they were instead different modes of one God.

- Dynamic monarchianism: the early church heresy that viewed the Holy Spirit as being little more than a divine influence

Essay Questions

Short

1. What terminology did the Cappadocian Fathers develop to explain the relationship between the Holy Spirit and the other members of the Trinity? What did their contribution accomplish?

2. What is the illumination of the Spirit? What does this doctrine safeguard, and what does it combat?

3. What is the difference between Pentecostalism, the charismatic movement, and third wave evangelicalism?

Long

1. One effect of the Reformers' connection between Spirit and Word was Calvin's doctrine of the witness of the Spirit. What did he mean by this? What did Wesley add to the doctrine of the Spirit? Compare and contrast his understanding to Calvin's notion of the internal witness of the Spirit.

Quiz

1. (T/F) The church in the East believes that the Spirit proceeds both from the Father and the Son, while the West believes him to proceed from the Father only.

2. (T/F) The Cappadocian fathers were known for their denial of the deity of the Holy Spirit and were, thus, exiled for their teachings.

3. (T/F) The original Nicene Creed affirmed the procession of the Spirit from both the Father and the Son.

4. (T/F) From the beginning of the church, baptism was done in the name of the Father, the Son, and the Holy Spirit.

5. (T/F) Dynamic monarchianism had a much greater influence on the early church than did modalistic monarchianism.

6. At the Council of _____, the church agreed to anathematize those who taught that the Holy Spirit is a creature.

   a) Ephesus
   b) Constantinople
   c) Alexandria
   d) Chalcedon

7. _____ argued that Christians could not be partakers of God if the Spirit were a created being. Athanasius further argued that both the Son and the Spirit are *homoousios* — of the same substance — with the Father and the Son.

   a) Athanasius
   b) Arius

    c) Eusebius of Caesarea
    d) Albert Schweitzer

8. _____ spoke of how the illuminating work of the Holy Spirit is necessary if Christians are to understand Scripture. He further distinguished between the Spirit's work of inspiration and illumination; whereas the Spirit inspired the writers of Scripture to write, he also illumines the minds of the readers of Scripture to understand.

    a) John Calvin
    b) Martin Luther
    c) Anselm
    d) John Owen

9. _____ originated the early church heresy called dynamic monarchianism.

    a) Zephyrinus
    b) Praxeas
    c) Origen
    d) Theodotus

10. _____ provided a systematic formulation of the Pentecostal-charismatic doctrine in his *Renewal Theology*. He taught the reality of two distinguishable experiences of the Holy Spirit, the last being a powerful second blessing and outpouring of the Holy Spirit that comes after a believer's salvation. He, furthermore, taught that the phenomenon of speaking in tongues accompanied these second blessings.

    a) C. Peter Wagner
    b) J. Rodman Williams
    c) Charles Fox Parham
    d) William J. Seymour

ANSWER KEY

1. F, 2. F, 3. F, 4. T, 5. F, 6. C, 7. A, 8. D, 9. D, 10. B

CHAPTER 21

Election and Reprobation

You Should Know

- Predestination is one of the most important yet contentious doctrines with which the church has dealt with in its history.

- Ignatius spoke of the synergistic cooperation between God and man in salvation. A serious challenge to this idea of cooperation came from Pelagius; he denied that man is born with a corrupt nature. Men only fall into sin if they choose to, but they have graciously been enabled by nature not to do so. Augustine countered Pelagius and refuted his theology.

- Origen emphasized God's role in hardening hearts. He further spoke of God's work of salvation being greater than man's, though he still left room for man's cooperation.

- The Council of Orange convened to address the conflict between Augustinianism, Pelagianism, and semi-Pelagianism. The council clearly stood against Pelagianism and opposed the idea of reprobation, which was an aspect of Augustinianism. In the end, the council agreed on a position most closely in line with Augustinianism.

- John Calvin affirmed predestination to be a part of God's eternal and unchanging decree and according to his gracious and free decision. Moreover, this election is individual. There are two types of individuals — elect and reprobate. Election or reprobation is assigned to the individual by God's decree.

- John Wesley rejected the Calvinistic doctrine of predestination. He acknowledged election to be a biblical idea; he affirmed two types. The first concerned the unconditional election of men to do some particular work in the world. The second concerned the conditional election of men to eternal happiness.

- Jacob Arminius opposed John Calvin's views on predestination. While affirming election, he argued that predestination is based on God's foreknowledge of those who will believe. He rejected both supralapsarianism and sublapsarianism. His views would be expressed in the *Five Articles of the Remonstrants*.

- Karl Barth claimed that Jesus is the divine election of grace. Indeed, Jesus is the electing God and the elected man. As the electing God, Jesus elects all humanity in himself. As the elected man, Jesus is not just one of the elect but *the* elect of God. Jesus stands above all humanity as the one who is originally and properly the elect. God's electing grace of all people meant that every person — even the one who persists in his rejection of God — will be saved. Thus, Barth was charged with embracing universalism.

- In general, the Reformed or Calvinist perspective has argued for a(n) unconditional view of election.

- In general, the Wesleyan or Arminian perspective has argued for a(n) conditional view of election.

Essay Questions

Short

1. What according to Aquinas is the basis of predestination? Explain.

2. What are some of the biblical texts that Calvin used to articulate his understanding of predestination, and what conclusions did he draw from them?

3. According to Arminius, what is the ultimate basis for God's decision to elect a person or not?

Long

1. How does Pelagius understand free will and predestination? How is the position of Augustine different? How did Augustine's understanding of predestination affect his understanding of the church?

Quiz

1. (T/F) The early church generally spoke of divine predestination in terms of being based on divine foreknowledge.

2. (T/F) Most evangelicals have followed the teaching of Karl Barth concerning the doctrines of election and reprobation.

3. (T/F) Augustine claimed that predestination includes election of some to eternal life and reprobation of others to eternal damnation.

4. (T/F) John Calvin rejected the idea of double predestination, that is, that there are two types of individuals — elect and reprobate — and that God decrees whether an individual will go to heaven or hell.

5. (T/F) John Wesley affirmed the Calvinistic doctrine of predestination.

6. _____ is the view that the decree of predestination was logically prior to the decree to create human beings and the decree to permit the fall of Adam.

    a) Prelapsarianism
    b) Infralapsarianism
    c) Sublapsarianism
    d) Supralapsarianism

7. _____ is the sovereign decision of God before creation to pass over some persons, in sorrow deciding not to save them and to punish them for their sins, and thereby to manifest his justice.

    a) Reprobation
    b) Election
    c) Predestination
    d) Foreknowledge

Election and Reprobation | 89

8. Concerning the issue of the freedom or bondage of the will, Martin Luther faced off against _____, who championed a limited human freedom whereas Luther maintained that there is no free will in man.

   a) John Calvin
   b) Philipp Melanchthon
   c) Huldrych Zwingli
   d) Erasmus

9. _____ rejected foreknowledge as the basis of predestination but instead associated love with God's election of people. He rejected the idea that man has anything to do with the cause of predestination. He further made a distinction between the decree and the actualization of predestination. He denied that predestination can be furthered by the prayers of the saints. Nevertheless, such prayers are the means that God has predestined and appointed to help the elect move toward the salvation to which God has predestined them.

   a) Thomas Aquinas
   b) Jacob Arminius
   c) John Cassian
   d) Justin Martyr

10. _____ denied that man is born with a corrupt nature. Men only fall into sin if they choose to, but they have graciously been enabled by nature not to do so.

    a) Praxeas
    b) Augustine
    c) Pelagius
    d) Anselm

ANSWER KEY

1. T, 2. F, 3. T, 4. F, 5. F, 6. D, 7. A, 8. D, 9. A, 10. C

CHAPTER 22

Regeneration, Conversion, and Effective Calling

You Should Know

- From its inception the church has associated regeneration and conversion with the proclamation of the gospel, the work of the Holy Spirit, the effective call, repentance, faith, and baptism.

- Tatian's conversion came from a study in which he contrasted the contradictory and unethical writings of the Greeks and Romans with the Scripture.

- Theophilus was converted through the reading of the Prophets.

- Cyprian noted that his conversion came as he pondered baptism. Cyprian, thus, came to believe that baptism regenerates. This belief would come to be closely associated with infant baptism. Augustine would come to endorse such a view, though his conversion was quite dissimilar to his own theology.

- Through the influence of Ambrose, Augustine forsook his heretical Manichaeism and his sexually immoral life and became a theologian and leader of the church.

- Pelagius believed in such a view of human free will that man is able to choose what is right or to choose what is wrong. Because no one is born with a corrupt nature or the tendency to sin, believers are able to live without sin. This, of course, stood against the church's traditional teaching of original sin that sinful man is in need of regeneration, faith, repentance, and baptism.

- The medieval church expanded through miraculous conversions of the pagans.

- John Calvin served to resurrect Augustine's teachings on the difference between a general and a special call to salvation — the general or universal call being extended to all men and the special or effective call being extended only to the elect. Those who receive this latter call always come to Christ for salvation.

- As a result of Arminian theology, many modern churches taught a kind of grace that is common to all unbelievers, is effective in overcoming the effects of original sin, and enables people to respond to God's work in salvation. This prevenient grace renders any special call to salvation unnecessary, since the same grace is extended to every person.

- As a part of Arminian theology, many modern churches taught a kind of grace called prevenient grace that is common to all unbelievers; it is effective in overcoming the effects of original sin and enables people to respond to God's work in salvation. This grace renders any special call to salvation unnecessary, since the same grace is extended to every person.

Essay Questions

Short

1. What were the two types of calling according to Augustine? Why did he emphasize the importance of a divine calling to salvation?

2. How did Calvin reconcile the practice of infant baptism and the necessity of faith for conversion? To what biblical precedent did he appeal?

3. How did the Anabaptists break from the standard understanding of baptism held by Catholics as well as many Protestants?

Long

1. Summarize and explain both prevenient grace and common grace. What is the difference between each of these graces?

Quiz

1. (T/F) Protestants have historically affirmed baptismal regeneration.

2. (T/F) Up until the Reformation, infant baptism — with its regenerating power — was the official rite of the church.

3. (T/F) Charles Finney's emphasis on the monergistic work of God in salvation led him to emphasize miraculous and divine means — rather than human means — in bringing about a revival

4. (T/F) Jonathan Edwards affirmed a twofold notion of grace, common grace and special grace. Edwards' notion of common grace concerned the grace that had to do with God's common assistance to all humanity in areas of morality. Special grace functions to bring about conversion.

5. (T/F) Millard Erickson rejected the logical priority of regeneration to conversion, arguing that the logical order is conversion and then regeneration. He argued that repentance and faith are the conditions that are necessary for regeneration. Thus, he believed the logical order to be special calling — conversion — regeneration.

6. _____ spoke of two calls — one that goes out to all people and does not result in salvation and a second that goes out only to the elect and does result in salvation. All those who are recipients of this second sort of grace do definitely come to faith in Christ.

   a) Augustine
   b) John Cassian
   c) Pelagius
   d) Jacob Arminius

7. Saxon pagans were converted to Christ as a result of an encounter between the one true God of the Bible and the Saxon god _____.

   a) Ashur
   b) Thor
   c) Chemosh
   d) Ares

8. During the Reformation, _____ served to resurrect Augustine's teachings on the difference between a general and a special call to salvation — the general or universal call being extended to all men and the special or effective call being extended only to the elect.

   a) Thomas Cranmer
   b) Michael Servetus
   c) John Calvin
   d) John Knox

9. Disagreement over the role of human will in conversion continued to be a source of major disagreement during the Middle Ages. _____ took issue with Augustine's perspective, insisting on God's work in assisting the will in something of a divine-human cooperation.

   a) Thomas Aquinas
   b) John of Damascus
   c) John Cassian
   d) John Duns Scotus

10. _____ believed in baptismal regeneration in the case of infants, though not in adults. However, all infants eventually grow up to reject the grace of God and must be born again as adults. Thus, infant baptism, though effective at the time, eventually loses its salvific power as the infants fall away. As adults, they must be born again — again.

    a) Jacob Arminius
    b) Martin Luther
    c) Huldrych Zwingli
    d) John Wesley

ANSWER KEY

1. F, 2. T, 3. F, 4. T, 5. T, 6. A, 7. B, 8. C, 9. C, 10. D

CHAPTER 23

Justification (Right Legal Standing before God)

You Should Know

- The church has historically believed justification to be one aspect of God's work of salvation.

- Augustine's theology stood in opposition to that of Pelagius, who believed grace to be an external help for people and denied the effects of original sin on humanity.

- In Augustine's scheme, prevenient grace prepares the individual for justification, justifying grace accomplishes justification for the individual, and persevering grace works throughout the process of justification so as to preserve it.

- Thomas Aquinas set forth the medieval Roman Catholic notion of justification and its corollaries of grace, human effort, and merit. He taught that one progresses or moves from a state of unrighteousness to righteousness over time. Divine resources are needed to accomplish this transition. Man can merit salvation through his works, though grace is needed to perform these works. Thus, Aquinas taught the need for synergy and human cooperation in obtaining salvation.

- On October 31, 1517, Martin Luther nailed his Ninety-Five Theses to the door of the Castle Church in Wittenberg in response to the Roman Catholic use of indulgences. Little did he know that his contention would spark a revolution over the doctrine of justification.

- Popularized by N. T. Wright, the "new perspective" on Paul and justification came to the fore at the turn of the third millennium. This perspective was not about sinners being made right with God, but rather about identifying the true members of the covenant community.

- Because many deceased saints have exceeded the requirement of their debt, according to the Roman Catholic Church, merit has been stored up in the treasury of the saints. Thus, indulgences could be obtained, and merit could be allocated for the deceased.

- Condign merit: a real merit of worthiness that is accomplished by a righteous person through divine grace

- Congruous merits: not strictly merits but are rather human works reckoned as merits, because in doing them, people do what is in them to do

- Purgatory: a place for the dead whose souls need further cleansing from venial sins. After a time of purification, the soul is transferred to heaven; those Christians who are still alive can provide help for those who have died and are in this place by offering prayers, masses, and alms on their behalf.

Essay Questions

Short

1. How did Augustine understand the relationship between faith, justification, righteousness, and merit?

2. Explain Luther's distinction between alien righteousness and proper righteousness. How does it differ from Aquinas's idea of infused righteousness?

3. How does Wright revise the traditional understanding of justification by faith?

Long

1. Explain the Roman Catholic position that insists human works that form the basis of justification are works that grow out of

regeneration. Why did Calvin find this position insufficient? How does Calvin relate justification by faith alone, excluding all good works, to the necessity for good works?

Quiz

1. (T/F) Clement of Rome taught that a man can bring himself to be justified apart from God's grace.

2. (T/F) In the *Letter to Diognetus*, justification is placed in the context of the removal of sins and the gift of the righteousness of Christ.

3. (T/F) In order to address the issue of fatalism, some spoke of justification within the context of free will and self-determination. Theophilus, for example, discussed the doctrine in light of merit, saying that anyone who desires salvation in their human freedom can obtain it.

4. (T/F) Luther distinguished between alien righteousness and man's proper righteousness. The latter was the basis for the former

5. (T/F) Charles Finney not only rejected the traditional notion of justification as a forensic or judicial proceeding but also denied the imputation of Christ's righteousness to sinners.

6. Augustine taught that _____ is a divine grace that prepares people for justification.

   a) Common grace
   b) Prevenient grace
   c) Justifying grace
   d) Persevering grace

7. Augustine taught that _____ is a divine grace that allows the believer to continue in a state of faith, leading to ultimate salvation.

   a) Common grace
   b) Prevenient grace
   c) Justifying grace
   d) Persevering grace

8. Augustine taught that _____ is a divine grace that belongs to the natural realm.

   a) Common grace
   b) Prevenient grace
   c) Justifying grace
   d) Persevering grace

9. Augustine taught that _____ is a divine grace that accomplishes the act of justification for the individual. Only those whom God has predestined are the recipients of this grace.

   a) Common grace
   b) Prevenient grace
   c) Justifying grace
   d) Persevering grace

10. Popularized by _____, the "new perspective" on Paul and justification came to the fore at the turn of the third millennium. This perspective was not about sinners being made right with God, but rather about identifying the true members of the covenant community.

    a) Roger Olson
    b) Thomas Schreiner
    c) Mark Seifrid
    d) N. T. Wright

ANSWER KEY

1. F, 2. T, 3. T, 4. F, 5. T, 6. B, 7. D, 8. A, 9. C, 10. D

CHAPTER 24

Sanctification (Growth in Likeness to Christ)

You Should Know

- The church has historically believed that growth in Christian maturity is part of the believer's experience in salvation. This work of sanctification is a progressive work of God's grace that makes man freer from sin and more like Christ.

- Early writers following the apostolic era believed that progress in Christian maturity is necessary evidence for one's relationship with Christ.

- When the persecution of the church ended at the close of the fourth century, celibacy replaced martyrdom as the highest calling for believers to follow. Thus, the order of virgins became an established part of the church. This naturally flowed into what would become monasticism, which would become the lifestyle of the most serious-minded believers.

- The Franciscans, followers of St. Francis of Assisi, made three vows — poverty, obedience, and celibacy — as a part of Francis' *Rule*. The Franciscans were joined by the Dominicans and the Augustinians as mendicant or begging orders.

- Whereas the Reformers believed growth in sanctification to be the lifelong pursuit of believers, Rome emphasized the need to progress in obtaining greater levels of justification. Whereas Catholics generally took a mystical approach to sanctification, Protestants focused on Christ's work of salvation, the Word, and the Spirit of God.

- In contrast to the historical position that sanctification cannot occur in this lifetime, John Wesley championed a new position that would come to be called Christian perfectionism. Wesley believed this Christian perfection to be attainable for all believers in this lifetime. While he did not believe Christians to ever be free of ignorance, mistakes, infirmities, and temptation, he affirmed that Christians can be free from outward and voluntary sin.

- Thomas à Kempis was a member of the *Devotio Moderna*, a movement that consisted of laypeople who gathered themselves into a community that resembled monastic order. However, its participants did not take monastic vows. He rejected the sterility of the scholastic theology of his time and charged his readers to follow Jesus in humility, love for God and others, virtue, and contempt for the praises of the world. Moreover, he emphasized the need for more than intellectual learning; holiness of life was of equal importance.

- The elevation of the celibate lifestyle confused the layperson, communicating the wrong idea of how to live a holy life. Indeed, the layperson came to believe that he could not please God unless he was celibate. To counteract this pattern of thought, the *Augsburg Confession* emphasized the rightness and purity of marriage for anyone who cannot endure the single life. Thus, marriage was not sinful, and celibacy was not forced. At the heart of the confession's rejection of the monastic lifestyle was its rejection of the doctrine of justification by grace through faith alone in Jesus Christ.

- Various types of monasticism began to develop during the early church, including anchoritism and cenobitism. This kind of lifestyle would become the lifestyle choice of the most serious-minded believers.

- During the early church, Clement of Alexandria taught that the Christian could arrive at some state of sinlessness. That is, he believed one could come to a place where he is not affected by temptation. Nevertheless, he also said that he knew of no one who is perfect in all things at the same time. To him, only Christ Jesus was perfect.

Essay Questions

Short

1. How did Tertullian express the dual necessity that Christians be both active in the world yet separate from its sin?

2. What contribution did the monastic orders make to the practice of spirituality in the Middle Ages?

3. What did Wesley mean by Christian perfectionism and how did he protect it from misunderstanding? What Scriptural passages did he use to support his view?

Long

1. How did Calvin apply his doctrine of sanctification to pastoral ministry? How are his views similar to Augustine's? Summarize and explain both of their positions.

Quiz

1. (T/F) Augustine believed that Christians would never have complete victory over sin in this lifetime.

2. (T/F) The Keswick approach to sanctification taught that the normal Christian life is one of uniform sustained victory over known sin, rather than constant defeat. The movement emphasized the "abundant life" promised by Christ and believed it to be both instantaneous and progressive.

3. (T/F) Cyprian insisted that Scripture teaches the impossibility of perfection.

4. (T/F) Justin Martyr believed that progress in Christian maturity was necessary evidence for one's relationship with Christ.

5. (T/F) Whereas the Roman Catholic Church believed growth in sanctification to be the lifelong pursuit of believers, the Protestant Reformers emphasized the need to progress in obtaining greater levels of justification.

6. (T/F) The church has always considered celibacy a strange and unholy lifestyle.

7. _____ taught that Christians should not completely withdraw from and separate themselves from the world.
   a) Tertullian
   b) Tatian
   c) Clement of Alexandria
   d) Cyprian

8. _____ philosophy, which encouraged the denigration of anything physical and material while emphasizing the goodness in the spiritual and immaterial, had a large impact on the doctrine of sanctification in the early church.
   a) Aristotelian
   b) Epicurean
   c) Platonic
   d) Stoic

9. Many early Christians practiced a lifestyle of _____ in an attempt to separate themselves from the world and become holy.
   a) Pietism
   b) Perfectionism
   c) Masochism
   d) Asceticism

10. With the cessation of the mass persecution of the church at the close of the fourth century, _____ replaced martyrdom as the highest calling for believers to follow.
    a) Marriage
    b) Pastoral ministry
    c) Asceticism
    d) Celibacy

ANSWER KEY

1. T, 2. T, 3. T, 4. T, 5. F, 6. F, 7. A, 8. C, 9. D, 10. D

CHAPTER 25

The Perseverance of the Saints (Remaining a Christian)

You Should Know

- The church has historically been divided over the doctrine of the perseverance of the saints and its corollary, eternal security or the assurance of salvation.

- Augustine provided the most thorough and systematic formulation of the doctrine in the early church. He believed perseverance to be a gift of God, a gift that cannot be lost. Nevertheless, no one in this life can know for sure if he has this gift, at least not until his life is finished.

- Thomas Aquinas's view of perseverance was closely tied to his view on meriting eternal life, which included a view of cooperation between the grace of God and human effort. Because of man's overall corruption, certainty of perseverance is not possible even for the redeemed.

- Martin Luther rejected the notion that God would have his children remain uncertain and in doubt about their salvation. He blamed feelings of doubt not only on Satan but also on the Catholic Church, which he denounced for abusing the confidence of conscience-stricken people.

- Regarding perseverance, Thomas Schreiner and Ardel Canday focused on the question of how God's warnings and admonitions relate to his promises of assured salvation and concluded that the two notions are compatible; the warnings function so as to continually preach the gospel in the lives of Christians, calling them to continued faithfulness in Christ.

- For Irenaeus, an emphasis on fearing the loss of salvation functioned as a preventative against the sin of pride.

- In general, Arminianism maintains that genuine Christians can apostatize and fall away from true faith, but that Christians may possess some level of assurance as they focus on the reality of the present state of grace.

- Many during the early church believed that sins committed after one's baptism could not be forgiven.

- In response to the view of John Wesley, that believers may fall away and be cut off between their special calling and glorification, Calvinists responded by appealing to the *ordo salutis*.

- The Calvinist perspective concerning the doctrine of perseverance that would be articulated in the *Canons of Dort* in response to Arminius' *Remonstrants* would affirm the Reformers' position.

Essay Questions

Short

1. What biblical texts did Augustine use to support his understanding of perseverance? How did Aquinas differ from Augustine in his understanding of perseverance?

2. According to the *Westminster Confession of Faith*, at what point may the believer attain assurance of salvation? Why did it adopt the position that it did?

3. How does Carson use the notion of "inauthentic faith" to explain perseverance and apostasy from a compatibilist perspective?

Long

1. According to Calvin, what is the basis of assurance? How is his position different from that of Aquinas? How did Arminius and the

Remonstrants deviate from Calvinism on the topic of assurance and perseverance?

Quiz

1. (T/F) The church has historically been united over the doctrine of the perseverance of the saints and its corollary, eternal security or the assurance of salvation.

2. (T/F) Martin Luther affirmed the possibility of assurance of salvation for believers in this lifetime.

3. (T/F) John Calvin rooted perseverance in his understanding of predestination and election.

4. (T/F) In general, Arminianism has suggested that believers will definitely persevere in the Christian faith and that genuine believers may possess the confidence that they will continue as believers throughout their life and will one day go to heaven.

5. (T/F) Thomas Aquinas' view of perseverance was closely tied to his view on meriting eternal life, which included a view of cooperation between the grace of God and human effort.

6. During the Middle Ages, _____ taught that perseverance required not only habitual grace but also sustaining grace.

   a) Thomas Aquinas
   b) Anselm
   c) John Duns Scotus
   d) John of Damascus

7. The Council of _____ condemned the doctrine of assurance as a heresy.

   a) Constantinople
   b) Nicea
   c) Trent
   d) Chalcedon

8. _____ argued from the Wesleyan-Arminian perspective, saying that the existence of warning passages in Scripture must indicate the possibility of a believer's failure to persevere.

a) I. Howard Marshall
b) D. A. Carson
c) Ardel Canday
d) Robert Shank

9. _____ believed doubting one's salvation to be a heinous sin against God. Instead of doubting, he encouraged believers to trust God and his Word and that their sin has been placed on Christ.

a) John Wesley
b) Charles Wesley
c) I. Howard Marshall
d) Martin Luther

10. _____ provided the most thorough and systematic formulation of the doctrine of the perseverance of the saints in the early church.

a) Irenaeus
b) Tertullian
c) Athanasius
d) Augustine

ANSWER KEY

1. F, 2. T, 3. T, 4. F, 5. T, 6. A, 7. C, 8. A, 9. D, 10. D

CHAPTER 26

The Church: Its Nature, Its Marks, and Its Purposes

You Should Know

- The Nicene Creed defined the church in terms of four characteristics: oneness, holiness, catholicity, and apostolicity.

- The church was further described by Tertullian, Methodius, and Cyprian as the mother of all faithful followers of Christ. Cyprian would go so far as to say that "there is no salvation outside of the church."

- With the rise of the Roman emperor Constantine in the fourth century, and his legalization of the church, the church began a new relationship with the state. This relationship allowed the state to exercise authority over the theology and practice of the church.

- The Donatists insisted that the church is truly and completely holy and is, thus, composed only of genuine believers. The Donatists, however, believed themselves to be the only holy and catholic church. In the end, Augustine condemned the Donatists as heretics and charged them to come back to the one holy and catholic church.

- Thomas Aquinas suggested that the church had three divisions: one on earth, another in heaven, and a third in purgatory.

- Both Martin Luther and John Calvin emphasized God's Word and the sacraments as the key marks of a true church.

- Regenerate church membership, believer's baptism, a church covenant, the church as a visible spiritual kingdom, local church autonomy, and congregational polity were all characteristics of Baptist ecclesiology.

- William Carey, known as the "father of Protestant missions," was influential in confronting churches that were hardened to considering their role in the evangelization of the people of the world.

- Beginning in the early seventeenth century, a new church — the Baptist church — offered a new ecclesiology that promoted the need for regenerate church membership. As the founding leaders of this church, John Smyth and Thomas Helwys both insisted that regeneration was a prerequisite to both baptism and subsequent church membership.

- J. N. Darby and Lewis Sperry Chafer developed what would be called dispensationalism, a new ecclesiology that drew a strong distinction between the Old and the New Testaments and made a complete separation between the remnant of the Jewish people and the church.

Essay Questions

Short

1. Why did Augustine make a distinction between the visible and the invisible church?

2. Which two (and sometimes three) marks of the church became dominant in Protestantism?

3. What changes in Roman Catholic ecclesiology were brought about by the Second Vatican Council?

Long

1. Summarize and explain the four characteristics of the church according to the Nicene Creed.

Quiz

1. (T/F) The church has historically affirmed and has been united over the belief that the church originated at Pentecost.

2. (T/F) Martin Luther listed seven marks of a true church. The first three, which regarded the importance of God's Word and the ordinances, became the focal points of the Lutheran understanding of the church.

3. (T/F) The visible church, according to Aquinas, was composed of a mixture of believers and nonbelievers.

4. (T/F) To bolster their authority, the Roman Catholic Church added two attributes to the church's essence — infallibility and indefectibility.

5. (T/F) Pentecostalism and the charismatic movement stand as the catalyst for the greatest expansion of the church in its history.

6. The church was often referred to as the _____ of all faithful followers of Christ.
    a) Father
    b) Mother
    c) Brother
    d) Sister

7. The _____ were against personal involvement in the civil government and would have nothing to do with the state churches — the Catholic Church and magisterial Protestant churches.
    a) Lutherans
    b) Anabaptists
    c) Presbyterians
    d) Anglicans

8. The _____ insisted that the church is truly and completely holy and is, thus, composed only of genuine believers. They, however, believed themselves to be the only holy and catholic church. In the end, they were condemned as heretics and were encouraged to come back to the one holy and catholic church.

a) Novatianists
b) Montanists
c) Docetists
d) Donatists

9. _____ is known for saying, "There is no salvation outside of the church."

a) Tertullian
b) Cyprian
c) Augustine
d) Methodius

10. _____ suggested that the church had three divisions: one on earth, another in heaven, and a third in purgatory.

a) Irenaeus
b) Martin Luther
c) Thomas Aquinas
d) Augustine

ANSWER KEY

1. F, 2. T, 3. F, 4. T, 5. T, 6. B, 7. B, 8. D, 9. B, 10. C

CHAPTER 27

Church Government

You Should Know

- The church has historically held variant views when it comes to church polity.

- The responsibilities given to the elders in the early church included leading the church, teaching sound doctrine, shepherding the church, and praying for the church.

- Ignatius proposed a new form of church government, one with a three-tiered authority structure: the overseer/bishop, the presbyter/elder, and the deacon. Ignatius elevated the office of one solitary bishop over the office of elder in terms of authority, with the office of deacon under both the bishop and the elder.

- The most important development during the Middle Ages was the expansion of the powers of the papacy.

- Following John Calvin, the *Westminster Assembly for Church Government* made a distinction between different levels of church government, involving the *Directory*, which called for the presbytery at the local level, the classis at the regional level, and the synod at the national level.

- A. H. Strong argued for a congregational government with a single pastor leading the church. He believed that while the New Testament does permit a plurality of pastors, the text does not require plural eldership in every case.

- The growing problems that existed within the papacy during the medieval period led to the Great Schism, a time when two popes vied for authority — one in Avignon and one in Rome.

- Calvin broke with the three-tiered authority structure and suggested rather that the church should be ruled by presbyters — a presbyterian government.

- The Church of England broke away from the Roman Catholic Church, though it kept an episcopalian form of church government.

Essay Questions

Short

1. In the threefold model of church governance, what is the role of the deacon?

2. What different interpretations of Matthew 16:15–19 did Cyprian and Pope Stephen give, and what was at stake?

3. What is the governing structure of the Church of England? How is it similar to and different from the Roman Catholic Church?

Long

1. What were the four offices of the church, according to Calvin? Why is his mode of church governance called *presbyterian*? What is the difference between a presbyterian form of government and a congregational form of government? What developments did the *Westminster Confession of Faith* introduce into Calvin's ecclesiology?

Quiz

1. (T/F) Martin Luther rebelled against the authority of the papacy, suggesting rather that pastors are the rightful leaders of congregations.

2. (T/F) Origen argued for the biblical legitimacy of female deaconesses by pointing to the example of Phoebe.

3. (T/F) The term *elder* was used interchangeably with presbyters, overseers, bishops, and pastor-teachers in the New Testament and continued to be used in this way even as late as the end of the fourth century.

4. (T/F) During the Middle Ages, the papacy was known for its unusual holiness and moral uprightness, both in word and in deed.

5. (T/F) The leadership pattern presented in the early church was twofold: elders and deacons.

6. The specific responsibilities given to elders included leading the church, teaching sound doctrine, shepherding the church, and _____.

   a) Evangelizing the lost
   b) Maintenance of the church property
   c) Praying for the church
   d) Visitation

7. _____ sought to substantiate the three-tiered hierarchical structure by pointing to the old covenant priesthood, making parallels between the high priests, priests, and Levites with the bishops, elders, and deacons.

   a) Clement of Alexandria
   b) Clement of Rome
   c) Cyril of Alexandria
   d) Cyprian

8. Deacons and _____ were appointed to assist in the functioning and service of the church.

   a) Deaconesses
   b) Elders
   c) Children
   d) Unbelievers

9. Though it ultimately failed, the Council of _____ sought to assert the authority of general church councils over the authority of the papacy.

a) Constantinople
b) Trent
c) Constance
d) Chalcedon

10. _____ fled from the Church of England with his congregation to Holland. He would later articulate his ideas for what would become the congregational form of church government.

a) Robert Boone
b) John Smyth
c) Thomas Helwys
d) A. H. Strong

ANSWER KEY

1. T, 2. T, 3. T, 4. F, 5. T, 6. C, 7. B, 8. A, 9. C, 10. A

CHAPTER 28

Baptism

You Should Know

- The church has historically been obedient to Christ's command to baptize. However, there has been a great deal of disagreement over the doctrine.

- The word *sacrament* is associated with the Greek term *mystery*.

- In the early church, baptism was believed to have several purposes: the forgiveness of sins, deliverance from death, regeneration or the new birth, the gift of the Holy Spirit, the renunciation of Satan, and identification with Jesus Christ.

- Augustine employed his principle *ex opera operato* — literally, "by the work performed." Baptism is, thus, effective by the simple fact that it is administered.

- Hugh of Amiens rejected infant baptism, saying that it does not confer anything on little children because infants cannot have faith. Indeed, he believed that their age prevents them from believing. However, the church rejected Hugh's position.

- In the city of Zurich, Felix Manz, Conrad Grebel, and George Blaurock — the originators of the Anabaptist movement — rejected infant baptism and instead began baptizing adults, beginning with themselves.

- With the turn of the third millennium, a number of developments have led to less attention being paid to the historic doctrine of baptism, including cooperative evangelistic efforts, multidenominational allegiances, ecumenical missionary endeavors, and the united stance that has been taken against opponents of the gospel. The doctrine of baptism has, thus, been relegated to a position of secondary importance by many.

- Martin Luther did not oppose the church's practice of infant baptism. Instead, he linked it with the Word of God and faith. Baptism works forgiveness of sins, delivers from death and the devil, and gives eternal salvation to all who believe, as the Word and promise of God declare. It is not the water itself that saves, but the Word of God, which is with and in the water, and faith, which trusts in the Word of God in the water.

- John Calvin justified infant baptism on the analogy between the old covenant sign of circumcision and the new covenant sign of baptism. He believed that infant baptism marked the children of Christians as holy, different from the children of unbelievers. Moreover, he did not believe that infant baptism itself was regenerative; instead, he believed infants to be baptized into future repentance and faith.

- Huldrych Zwingli considered reserving baptism for believers. This opinion came from his view of the sacraments, that they are external signs by which people respond to what God has done. Against the common view of the relationship between original sin and infant baptism, he denied the idea that original sin can condemn the infant. Condemnation only comes to the child when he acts out of his corruption against the law of God, and one can only do that if he knows the law. However, he would eventually practice infant baptism after his confrontation with the Anabaptists.

Essay Questions

Short

1. What is the principle of *ex opere operato*?

2. How did Aquinas answer the question as to whether baptism was necessary for salvation?

3. How did Barth connect the baptism of the Holy Spirit and water baptism?

Long

1. Why did Anabaptists reject infant baptism? How did Zwingli's early theology of baptism contribute to this rejection? What was Calvin's twofold purpose of baptism? How did he relate this purpose to the topic of infant baptism?

Quiz

1. (T/F) Augustine believed that some outside the church would be saved and that many inside the church would be damned.

2. (T/F) The requirement of catechumens to undergo a period of catechesis prior to baptism stood in contrast to the New Testament practice for baptism.

3. (T/F) Tertullian rejected infant baptism and advocated baptizing only believers.

4. (T/F) During the Middle Ages, baptism was considered to be the preeminent sacrament.

5. (T/F) It is unclear as to whether the early church was or was not obedient to Christ's command to baptize.

6. In the city of _____, Felix Manz, Conrad Grebel, and George Blaurock — the originators of the Anabaptist movement — rejected infant baptism and instead began baptizing adults, beginning with themselves. City leaders did not tolerate the Anabaptists, but instead condemned their practices as heresy and sentenced them to death by drowning.
   a) Munich
   b) Rome
   c) Geneva
   d) Zurich

7. The _____ denied that water baptism should be observed; baptism was instead thought to be a spiritual thing — a baptism of the Spirit and fire.
   a) Baptists
   b) Methodists

c) Episcopalians
d) Quakers

8. _____ believed baptism to be the initiatory sacrament in which believers enter into covenant with God. It washes away the guilt of original sin and effects regeneration. He did not equate baptism with the new birth in the case of adults who are baptized, but he did in the case of infant baptism. However, he believed that infants eventually grow up to commit personal sin, reject the grace of God, and thus lose the eternal life given to them in baptism. This situation calls for them to be born again as adults.

   a) John Wesley
   b) Huldrych Zwingli
   c) Karl Barth
   d) Hugh of Amiens

9. Baptists administer the ordinance of baptism to believers by _____.

   a) Pouring
   b) Sprinkling
   c) Immersion
   d) Various means

10. _____ spoke of baptism, saying that it is something real signified by an outward washing, and a sacramental sign of inward justification. He rejected the necessity of immersion as the only proper mode for baptism, accepting both sprinkling and pouring. He further argued that baptism is essential for salvation in the sense that it must be something that is desired. That is, one is not saved if he does not desire it. However, if the person desires it but is unable to obtain it, he can obtain salvation on account of his desire.

    a) George Blaurock
    b) John Smyth
    c) Thomas Helwys
    d) Thomas Aquinas

ANSWER KEY

1. T, 2. T, 3. T, 4. F, 5. F, 6. D, 7. D, 8. A, 9. C, 10. D

CHAPTER 29

The Lord's Supper

You Should Know

- The church has historically been faithful to obey the Lord's command to observe the Lord's Supper. However, it has done so with various understandings of the meaning, purpose, and results of its observation.

- Cyprian emphasized the necessity for an individual to be a baptized believer before he is eligible to partake of the meal. Unbelievers were not welcome to partake in communion until they became Christians and were baptized.

- Augustine believed that God's grace was communicated through the sacraments no matter who dispenses them and no matter where they are dispensed. Thus, the sacraments of baptism and the Lord's Supper are necessary for salvation.

- Paschasius Radbertus affirmed the real presence of Christ in the elements. Before consecration, the elements are simply a figure of the bread and wine. However, after consecration, the elements are in reality the very body and blood of Jesus Christ.

- Thomas Aquinas presented a strong theological and philosophical explanation to support transubstantiation. In doing so, Aquinas set forth the definitive Roman Catholic perspective on the presence of Christ in the Eucharist.

- Huldrych Zwingli would face off with Martin Luther at the Marburg Colloquy in 1529. The debate included fifteen points of discussion; the two men were able to agree on fourteen of the points. However, the one point of disagreement served to widen the divide.

- John Wesley believed the Lord's Supper to be a means of conversion for unbelievers and a means of sanctification for believers. Baptists practiced "closed communion," restricting participation to only those believers who had been immersed in baptism.

- Consubstantiation: the view concerning the Lord's Supper that contends that the bread and the wine do not actually become the body and blood of Jesus Christ, but that the true body and blood of Christ are present "in, with, and under" the elements

- Transubstantiation: the view concerning the Lord's Supper that contends that the elements of the bread and the wine are changed in substance into Christ's body and blood

- Concomitance: the view that the entirety of Christ exists in each of the elements of the Lord's Supper

Essay Questions

Short

1. How did the early church understand Christ to be present in the Lord's Supper?

2. Explain Augustine's distinction between the sign and the grace signified, which he used to explain the sacraments.

3. What was the dispute between Radbertus and Ratramnus, and what were the consequences of their disagreement for the medieval church?

Long

1. What is transubstantiation, how is it related to Aristotle's distinction between substance and accidents, and on what grounds did Wycliffe attack it? What is meant by the term *consubstantiation*, and is it a fair label for Luther's theology of the Lord's Supper? Why did Zwingli say that the Lord's Supper is a memorial?

Quiz

1. (T/F) The *Didache* gives evidence that the early church continued observing the Lord's Supper after the apostolic period and that the Supper was to be reserved for baptized believers.

2. (T/F) John Hus questioned Rome's practice of communion in one kind, arguing from the conviction that the church should not follow custom but rather the example of Christ.

3. (T/F) The Anabaptists emphasized the need to be baptized as an infant before partaking of the Supper.

4. (T/F) According to Cyprian, an individual had to be a baptized believer before he was considered eligible to partake of the Lord's Supper. Unbelievers were not welcome to partake in communion until they became Christians and were baptized.

5. (T/F) John Wycliffe endorsed the Roman Catholic doctrine of transubstantiation.

6. _____ offered a critique of the "real presence" view. He appealed to the early church fathers. Specifically, he pointed to Ambrose, who believed Christ's body to have been resurrected and ascended into heaven, in an exalted and unchangeable state. Therefore, Christ cannot once again become a suffering victim in the Eucharist. Ultimately, he was forced by the church to repudiate his view.

   a) Thomas Aquinas
   b) Hugh of Amiens
   c) Berengar of Tours
   d) Paschasius Radbertus

7. According to _____, the Supper is an outward and visible sign of an invisible yet genuine grace. Moreover, the Supper is effective in communicating grace *ex opera operato* — literally, by the work performed.

   a) Irenaeus
   b) Cyprian
   c) Augustine
   d) Justin Martyr

8. At the Lateran Council in 1215, transubstantiation became the official position of the church. After the official decree at the Council, _____ presented a strong theological and philosophical explanation to support transubstantiation. In doing so, he set forth the definitive Roman Catholic perspective on the presence of Christ in the Eucharist.

   a) Thomas Aquinas
   b) Hugh of Amiens
   c) Berengar of Tours
   d) Paschasius Radbertus

9. During the ninth century, _____ affirmed the real presence of Christ in the elements. Before consecration, the elements are simply a figure of the bread and wine. However, after consecration, the elements are in reality the very body and blood of Jesus Christ. Though he experienced much resistance, his perspective of the real body and blood of Jesus was adopted by the church.

   a) Berengar of Tours
   b) Paschasius Radbertus
   c) Rabanus Maurus
   d) Hugh of Amiens

10. Augustine's belief that God's grace is communicated through the ordinances no matter where they are celebrated stood against the views and practices of the _____, who believed that sacraments were not valid unless they were observed inside the church.

    a) Donatists
    b) Novatianists
    c) Montanists
    d) Docetists

ANSWER KEY

1. T, 2. T, 3. F, 4. T, 5. F, 6. C, 7. C, 8. A, 9. B, 10. A

CHAPTER 30

Worship

You Should Know

- The church has historically gathered together for worship every Sunday, if not more frequently. Included historically in the worship of God have been such activities as praising and thanking God through song and prayer, reading and preaching the Word of God, celebrating the sacraments, interceding for needs, and giving financially.

- Following a set liturgy was a common practice for many churches. The Roman Mass — or the *Roman missal* — became a liturgical template for the church's worship services by the fifth century.

- Because of the developing doctrines of concomitance and communion in one kind, the Catholic Church began to give the bread but not the cup to the laity. According to the doctrine of concomitance, the Christian may receive all of Christ if he only takes one of the elements, since all of Christ is present in either element. Thus, the practice of communion in one kind became the norm.

- An important development of worship services that came during the twentieth century came through the Pentecostal/charismatic movement. Although the Spirit's leading often yielded the speaking of tongues during worship services, the characteristic element of Pentecostal worship was spontaneity.

- After failed attempts at reform, the English appointed the Westminster Assembly to reform the church. The group would produce *A Directory for the Public Worship of God*, which was to be the standard form for worship in the kingdoms of England, Scotland, and Ireland.

- Richard Baxter published *Reformation of the Liturgy*, which would come to be known as the *Savoy Liturgy* and represent the Puritan insistence that the proper worship of God must be governed by the regulative principle.

- Calvin was known for his use of the regulative principle for worship.

- It was the English Baptists who initiated the regular practice of singing hymns during the worship service. An important figure in this movement was Benjamin Keach, who sought to include the singing of a hymn to conclude the Lord's Supper. Over time, this practice was accepted by most church members, though some dissenters revolted and caused a split in the church. He defended himself against the revolt and even published hundreds of hymns.

Essay Questions

Short

1. What is Calvin's regulative principle and how did he apply it?

2. How did individualism and revivalism influence Baptist worship practices?

3. How did the charismatic movement influence mainline denominations?

Long

1. What are the key elements in Christian worship according to Justin Martyr? In what ways do you find them missing and evident within contemporary worship contexts?

Quiz

1. (T/F) John Calvin began his worship services with the public confession of sin.

2. (T/F) During the Middle Ages, few laypeople actually participated in the Eucharist; instead, they chose to adore the host — the transubstantiated body of Christ — that was held in the tabernacle after the Mass was over.

3. (T/F) The Roman Catholic Church critiqued the Reformers for their lack of emphasis on the preaching of the Word of God in worship.

4. (T/F) John Calvin's emphasis on liturgical worship would fade in the following centuries in both the Presbyterian and Reformed churches.

5. (T/F) The church has historically gathered together for worship every Sunday, if not more frequently.

6. Reverting back to a Calvinistic theology, _____ published the second book of prayer for the Anglican Church.

   a) Queen Mary
   b) Queen Elizabeth
   c) Henry VIII
   d) Edward VI

7. The first independent congregation to separate from Queen Elizabeth's Church of England was formed in the winter of 1580–81 by Robert Browne and _____ in Norwich. In pursuit of religious freedom, they led their congregation in a way distinctly different from the Anglican Church.

   a) John Owen
   b) Robert Harrison
   c) Thomas Helwys
   d) Benjamin Keach

8. The _____ required Catholics to participate in the Eucharist at least once per year.

   a) Council of Chalcedon
   b) Council of Trent
   c) Fourth Lateran Council
   d) Council of Constantinople

9. The _____ claimed to have received an inner light or inspiration, which would lead them into the worship of God. There was not a regulating principle. Instead, individuals apparently received inspiration of the Spirit.

    a) Methodists
    b) Anabaptists
    c) Amish
    d) Quakers

10. According to the doctrine of _____, the Christian may receive all of Christ if he only takes one of the elements, since all of Christ is present in either element.

    a) Spiritual presence
    b) Transubstantiation
    c) Consubstantiation
    d) Concomitance

ANSWER KEY

1. T, 2. T, 3. F, 4. F, 5. T, 6. B, 7. B, 8. C, 9. D, 10. D

CHAPTER 31

Christ's Return and the Millennium

You Should Know

- The church has historically placed its hope in the belief that God will intervene in the world to put an end to all opposition and ungodliness, reward his faithful followers, and make all things new. The church has further believed in the "second coming" of Jesus Christ.

- Four views are common in the discussion of the millennium: amillennialism, historic premillennialism, dispensational premillennialism, and postmillennialism.

- Early church fathers affirmed as a part of the "rule of faith" that Christ had two advents: one at his incarnation and another that would come at a future point when he would come from heaven with glory.

- The early church spoke of another important event that is associated with Christ's second coming: the reign of Christ upon the earth for a millennium. Many believed the millennium (Rev. 20:1–6) to speak of a literal one-thousand-year reign of Christ, one that begins immediately after his return—premillennialism.

- Augustine considered the one thousand years to extend from the first coming of Christ to the end of the world, to the second coming of Christ. Thus, for Augustine, there is no future millennium that the church looks forward to. Augustine's amillennial interpretation of the Scripture would become the dominant eschatological belief for over the next millennium.

- Reformation and post-Reformation theologians continued to affirm amillennialism.

- During the modern period, a third view arose to rival both amillennialism and premillennialism: postmillennialism. This position presented the view that Christ would return after the millennium. At this point, God would come in power, people everywhere would convert to Christ, governments would support the church, and Christianity would flourish in every respect. After a period of prosperity, Christ would return.

- The historic premilliennial position was challenged with a newer premillennial viewpoint. John Nelson Darby originated what has come to be known as dispensational premillennialism.

- As a part of his dispensational premillennial eschatology, William Blackstone petitioned the United States government to support the Jews, since he believed that the Jews must be restored to Palestine. He further contributed to the dispensational theology of the movement when he divided history into seven periods or "dispensations."

- The work of Johann Heinrich Alsted and Joseph Mede set the stage for premillennialism in the modern era. It could be said that they served to turn Protestant theology away from amillennialism and back to premillennialism.

Essay Questions

Short

1. What is the distinction made in the early church (and often since) between an imminent and an immediate return of Christ? How did the creative week of Genesis 1 affect the eschatological calculations of the early church?

2. Why were the Reformers largely opposed to premillennialism?

3. What were the seven dispensations discerned by theologians such as Blackstone and Scofield, and why did this approach become so popular among evangelicals?

Long

1. Summarize and explain each of the four views common in the discussion of the millennium, exploring how they arose as well as their strengths and weaknesses.

Quiz

1. (T/F) The church has historically believed in the "second coming" of Jesus Christ, a time in the future when Christ will make a personal, visible, sudden, and bodily return to the earth.

2. (T/F) Hippolytus interpreted the end-times vision of Daniel 7 to mean that the tribulation would precede the return of Christ. He further believed that the church would experience intense persecution during the period leading up to Christ's return.

3. (T/F) Charles Hodge and William G. T. Shedd defended premillennialism against amillennialism.

4. (T/F) Jonathan Edwards was a postmillennialist.

5. (T/F) Lewis Sperry Chafer contributed to the dispensational eschatological movement with his emphasis on a pretribulational rapture.

6. The early church placed the return of Christ _____ the period of great tribulation.
    a) At the midpoint of
    b) Before
    c) During
    d) After

7. _____ challenged amillennialism with his three-age scheme of the unfolding of history, with the first corresponding with the Old Testament, the second to the New Testament, and the third with a future spiritual understanding.
    a) John L. Girardeau
    b) Robert Harrison
    c) J. Rodman Williams
    d) Joachim Fiore

8. _____ considered the millennium to extend from the first coming of Christ to the second coming of Christ. Thus, he denied the idea that there is a future millennium that the church looks forward to. The resurrection is a spiritual one and applies both to the believers who are alive in Christ and to the dead who enjoy rest in heaven. However, the second resurrection is a dreadful reality for unbelievers. Unlike the first resurrection, the second is physical. His amillennial interpretation of the Scripture would become the dominant eschatological belief for over the next millennium.

   a) Augustine
   b) Cyprian
   c) Papias
   d) Lactantius

9. _____ originated what has come to be known as *dispensational premillennialism*. In this perspective, the church has not replaced Israel as the people of God. Instead, the two groups are distinct. Also, the church would escape the tribulation period and would be raptured. Indeed, the church would experience blessing through the rapture prior to the great tribulation; but Israel would receive the earthly blessing that would come in the millennium.

   a) William Blackstone
   b) John Nelson Darby
   c) C. I. Scofield
   d) Tim LaHaye

10. _____ ascribed to the position that the pope — or the papacy — was the Antichrist. Thus, he sought to destroy the Catholic Church for the sake of the true church.

    a) Thomas Aquinas
    b) Martin Luther
    c) Francis Turretin
    d) Charles Spurgeon

ANSWER KEY

1. T, 2. T, 3. F, 4. T, 5. T, 6. D, 7. D, 8. A, 9. B, 10. B

CHAPTER 32

The Final Judgment and Eternal Punishment

You Should Know

- From its beginning, the church has affirmed that there will be a final judgment of both believers and unbelievers.

- Origen introduced a controversial idea when he suggested that the transforming nature of God's punishment might cleanse each soul from evil, eventually restoring all fallen beings — angels, humans, and even Satan and his demons. Origen was the earliest church father charged with the heresy of universalism.

- Theologians and church leaders were not the only ones who affirmed and sought to describe the realities of eternal torment during the Middle Ages. Artists, poets, and writers, such as Michelangelo, Dante Alighieri, and John Milton all served to depict the loathsomeness of hell in their respective art forms.

- While Quenstedt believed that Christians will enjoy eternal life equally, he also affirmed that there will be "accessory rewards" — blessings that accompany eternal life — that believers will experience in varying degrees of blessing.

- Karl Barth argued for a universal salvation that comes as a result of God's grace through the work of Jesus Christ.

- Jonathan Edwards, known for his sermon "Sinners in the Hands of an Angry God," affirmed the historical teachings on the doctrines of the final judgment and eternal punishment.

- Conditional immortality: the view that claimed that, whereas Christians receive the gift of immortality from God (who alone possesses it), non-Christians do not; thus, their existence ends at death

- Universalism: the view that maintained that all people will eventually be saved by the love of God in Jesus Christ

- Annihilationism: the position that held that non-Christians will experience conscious punishment for a time after they die but eventually will be obliterated

Essay Questions

Short

1. How did Augustine describe eternal death? What objections to the doctrine of eternal punishment did Augustine confront? How did he respond? What Scripture did he use to support his own position?

2. How did Aquinas use Aristotle to support the doctrine of eternal divine punishment? How did Calvin understand the biblical language used to describe the final punishment of the wicked?

3. How did Schleiermacher reinterpret the doctrine of eternal punishment and final judgment?

Long

1. Summarize and explain the major views of final judgment presented in this session, exploring their strengths and weaknesses.

Quiz

1. (T/F) From its beginning, the church has affirmed that there will be a final judgment of believers but not unbelievers.

2. (T/F) Thomas Aquinas rejected the idea that God's punishment of the wicked is eternal. Instead, he believed that punishment must be temporary in order to be consistent with divine justice.

3. (T/F) Karl Barth argued for a universal salvation that comes as a result of God's grace through the work of Jesus Christ.

4. (T/F) Frederick Farrar argued that the church's hope for salvation was broader than the historical church doctrine allowed. He believed

this to be true because none of the general church councils laid down any doctrine concerning the eternal misery of the wicked.

5. _____ argued for the doctrine of annihilationism. While he acknowledged that the teaching was inconsistent with most of church history, he still believed that the teaching should be understood as a viable and biblically defensible option for Christians.

   a) Karl Barth
   b) William G. T. Shedd
   c) Robert Peterson
   d) John Stott

6. _____ introduced a controversial idea when he suggested that because God's punishment works to cleanse each soul from evil, God would eventually restore all fallen beings — angels, humans, and even Satan and his demons.

   a) Athenagoras
   b) Origen
   c) Justin Martyr
   d) Cyprian

7. _____ spoke of the first death as the separation of the soul and the body, and the second death as the uniting of the soul and the body in eternal death. In this latter death, people exist always *in* death — never living, never dead, but always dying. Death will be deathless.

   a) Origen
   b) John Stott
   c) Augustine
   d) Faustus Socinus

8. _____ believed that divine punishments cannot be ordained by God as reformative nor vengeful or retributive. He dismissed the traditional notion of a last judgment and did not allow for a final separation between believers and unbelievers. He further dismissed the doctrine of eternal damnation, saying that Jesus's discussion of an eternal hell was to be interpreted figuratively. In the end, he believed that there will one day be a universal restoration of all souls.

a) Friedrich Schleiermacher
b) Karl Barth
c) John Stott
d) William G. T. Shedd

9. _____ appealed to reason in his argument for "eternal unhappiness for the soul that rejects the supreme essence."

a) Augustine
b) Anselm
c) Papias
d) Thomas Aquinas

10. _____ cautioned against taking the biblical description of eternal fire literally. He believed rather that the biblical imagery should function to evoke a deep sense of the fury of God's might bearing down against the wicked.

a) Friedrich Schleiermacher
b) Martin Luther
c) Francis Turretin
d) John Calvin

CHAPTER 33

The New Heavens and New Earth

You Should Know

- From its beginning, the church has believed that after the final judgment believers will enter into full enjoyment of life in the presence of God forever, in a new heavens and a new earth.

- The early church believed in a series of events that would initiate the second coming: Christ's return, the defeat of Satan, the bodily resurrection of Christians, the thousand year reign of these believers with Christ on earth, the resurrection of the unbelievers after the millennium, the final judgment, and the establishment of the eternal state of heaven and hell.

- According to those in the early church, the end would be preceded by unmistakable signs, including a period of unprecedented wickedness, tumult, wars, and cosmic chaos.

- Thomas Aquinas affirmed that the world would be renewed in the same way that man would be renewed. An environment must be fitting for its inhabitants. Thus, if man is to be renewed, then the created order must be transformed into an existence that is suitable for the renewed human.

- The Reformed theologian Francis Turretin recognized the nonessential nature of the question of whether the created order would be annihilated or rehabilitated at the coming of the new heavens and the new earth. He further urged the allowance for disagreement between the two views.

- Wayne Grudem argued for the physical nature of the new heavens and the new earth, substantiating his position through the use of Scripture. Grudem sought to balance his view by also emphasizing the more important fellowship that will be enjoyed eternally between God and his people.

- For theologian A. A. Hodge, the divine teleology—God's purpose for human existence in the world—demanded that the new heavens and new earth would be thoroughly adapted for human existence.

- Friedrich Schleiermacher, with his redefinition of the Christian faith as God-consciousness, taught that there was no place for an external, physical transformation of the created order into a renewed world. Indeed, he believed that any notion of transformation is meaningless.

- Millard Erickson spoke of the perfect environment in which Christians will dwell at their glorification. He further spoke of heaven in terms of its physicality, while also addressing the hope of being in the presence of God. In fact, he spoke of the spiritual qualities of heaven to the neglect of the physical. Indeed, he spoke of heaven being more of a state than an actual place.

- Charles Hodge reaffirmed the traditional teaching on the doctrine and made his case using both Scripture and science. From his evidence, Hodge concluded that renovation rather than annihilation was the correct perspective. He, however, limited this renovation to the earth, rather than extending it to the entire universe.

Essay Questions

Short

1. What was the main point of dispute among theologians of the early church concerning the nature of the new heavens and new earth?

2. What speculative elements did Aquinas incorporate into his presentation of the doctrine of the new creation?

3. How did Calvin deal with passages that appear to indicate a complete destruction of the world and its replacement by a new heavens and new earth?

Long

1. How does Grudem employ the doctrines of the resurrection and the ascension to address the question of the nature of heaven?

Quiz

1. (T/F) Origen believed that the creation would not literally be destroyed but that it would rather be transformed.

2. (T/F) Tertullian denied the idea that the created order would be totally annihilated before the new heavens and new earth would be established.

3. (T/F) In general, eschatology was a matter of great significance and great discussion during the Middle Ages.

4. (T/F) While the church has agreed over the hope that exists for Christians, disagreement exists concerning how this final event will come about.

5. (T/F) The Reformers had very little to say about eschatology in general.

6. _____ denied the notion of the total annihilation of the current heavens and earth. Instead of the creation being annihilated, those things among which transgression has occurred will be renewed and flourish in an incorruptible state.
   a) Tertullian
   b) Irenaeus
   c) Melito of Sardis
   d) Quenstedt

7. _____ believed that God designed to elect and redeem a set number of human beings that would equal the number of fallen angels. God did this to restore the universe from the effects of sin. In order for the universe to be changed into something better, there-

fore, the total number of elect humans must be reached before the world could be restored.

    a) Anselm
    b) Origen
    c) Karl Barth
    d) Friedrich Schleiermacher

8. _____ affirmed that the world would be renewed in the same way that man would be renewed. An environment must be fitting for its inhabitants. Thus, if man is to be renewed, then the created order must be transformed into an existence that is suitable for the renewed human.

    a) Melito of Sardis
    b) Karl Barth
    c) Friedrich Schleiermacher
    d) Thomas Aquinas

9. During the modern era, _____ changed up the discussion and focused on the spiritual realities that are to come. He noted that the heavenly state for the Christian would be marked by sinless perfection, impeccability or indefectibility, mental happiness, and the personal presence of the mediator with his people.

    a) Millard Erickson
    b) Friedrich Schleiermacher
    c) William G. T. Shedd
    d) Francis Turretin

10. _____ made a case for the physical nature of the new heavens and the new earth, substantiating his position through the use of Scripture. He sought to balance his view by also emphasizing the more important fellowship that will be enjoyed eternally between God and his people.

    a) Friedrich Schleiermacher
    b) William G. T. Shedd
    c) Millard Erickson
    d) Wayne Grudem

ANSWER KEY

1. T, 2. F, 3. F, 4. T, 5. T, 6. B, 7. A, 8. D, 9. C, 10. D

Notes

www.ingramcontent.com/pod-product-compliance
Lightning Source LLC
LaVergne TN
LVHW032322080426
835508LV00046B/3360